REMEMBERING A GREAT
AMERICAN HERO
MARIAN ANDERSON

REMEMBERING A GREAT
AMERICAN HERO
MARIAN ANDERSON

"THE LADY FROM PHILADELPHIA"

EMILE HENWOOD

ISBN: Hardcover   978-1-6641-4967-0
              Softcover   978-1-6641-4966-3
              eBook   978-1-6641-4965-6

Print information available on the last page.

Rev. date: 12/26/2020

To order additional copies of this book, contact:
Xlibris
844-714-8691
www.Xlibris.com
Orders@Xlibris.com
816884

Contents

Foreword.. vii

Preface ix

Acknowledgments.. xiii

Chronology.. 1

End Notes 67

Appendix 69

Photographs 73

Foreword

Humility and generosity graciously harmonized in the remarkable life of Philadelphia's musical daughter, Marian Anderson. Her moving life story, with its profound fruitfulness and sweeping impact, has nearly been forgotten. But thanks to the loving efforts of Emile Henwood, her melodious life sings again.

Henwood demonstrates that Marian Anderson was, as his title asserts, "a great American Hero". Her life well modeled the benediction that flows from one who pursues excellence with a deep personal purpose. Indeed, she is an exemplar of a life well lived. The blessing of her life was not only a gift then but is needed now too in these times so marked by turmoil. People gravitated to Marian Anderson yesterday and will surely do so again today through this depiction of "The Lady from Philadelphia".

Marian Anderson's legacy is adorned by numerous accomplishments, countless admirers and a multitude of communities influenced by her trailblazing humanitarianism. This study captures and interconnects the multiple strands of her extraordinary life. Here, the ninety-six years of Marian Anderson's sojourn and their abiding impact unfold through a chronological narrative amply illustrated by engaging photos. This format enables readers, educators, researchers and perhaps even future screen writers to discover the multiform contours of her life.

A woman of faith, Anderson believed that with God, all things are possible. Her trust in the Lord's purposes for her life encouraged her to deploy her God-given talent of vocal genius with humility to overcome obstacles unimaginable today. Her talent extended beyond her musical prowess, as she displayed skills and interests as a fashion designer, seamstress, dark room photographer, farm gardener, cook, homemaker, furniture upholsterer, and lover of animals. Without children of her own, she steadfastly directed her love, attention, and generosity toward the welfare of the young.

In our fast-paced context it is often difficult to make reading a priority. Yet I am confident that I speak for the author when I assert that I hope you will return to this book often. It has been formatted and its contents compiled to enable most readers to complete a perusal in a sitting or two. The appendix offers twenty-three recommended titles for further research. And finally, be sure to visit the full-time epicenter of her curated collection – The National Marian Anderson Historical Society and Residence Museum in Philadelphia, Pennsylvania. Your visit there along with reading this engaging book by Emile Henwood will embed Marian Anderson in your heart bringing refreshing and uplifting music to your soul.

Dr. Peter A. Lillback,
President, Westminster Theological Seminary
President Emeritus, The Providence Forum
Philadelphia, Pennsylvania

Preface

This is a factual timeline compiled from many sources, a chronological commentary, with primary focus on significant events during and about the life of Marian E. Anderson (1897–1993).

In the fall of 2018, I had planned to attend the Marian Anderson Awards event that has been held annually at the Kimmel Center in my hometown of Philadelphia for the last twenty years. For reasons I cannot remember, I was curious and decided to attend. Unfortunately, that year's event was cancelled.

In my youth, I remembered hearing the name "Marian Anderson" but really knew little more than that she was a singer whom my parents and especially my paternal grandparents were very fond of. I decided to do a quick search for her on the internet. To my amazement, I got dozens of hits and started drilling down. I found it awfully hard to believe that one person could have accomplished everything I found.

I discovered there is a National Marian Anderson Historical Society, which is headquartered in the Anderson family's home, which is now an official historic residence museum—and the price of admission was only ten dollars with a personal tour guide! In March 2019, during my first visit, I was blown away by what I saw and learned about Marian Anderson.

This private Anderson family home-based museum is a repository of the largest collection of Marian Anderson's personal belongings and memorabilia, as well as the epicenter for authentic historical information about her life and legacy. The museum offers close-up inspection of hundreds of artifacts: Marian's beautiful performance gowns, clothing, accessories, tens of thousands of photographs, videos, recordings, jewelry, private pictures, and personal items, complete with lectures and guided tours (by appointment only). Visitors can discover how each artifact is connected to her life's story—over the span of a century—as a Philadelphian, as an artist and as an icon.

It took me a few more visits to begin to absorb what is there. In retrospect, this was just the tip of the iceberg. After each visit, I left with mixed feelings of awe, newfound respect, and embarrassment. How could I, having lived in Philadelphia for so long—not far from the very home Marian Anderson purchased in 1924, now a museum, in a neighborhood I went through frequently—have absolutely no idea that I was passing in the vicinity of such greatness? After reading Marian Anderson's autobiography, my hunger to know more led me to discover more than twenty other biographies, from excellent books for schoolchildren to several well-researched works by distinguished scholars. It is from the latter academic group that I have primarily drawn to compile and condense the information presented in this book.

There is a massive amount of historical information available about Marian Anderson, beyond the twenty-plus biographies, in her extensive personal papers at the University of Pennsylvania Library, the National Marian Anderson Historical Residence and Museum, various PBS documentaries, the Smithsonian Institution, the internet, and undocumented verbal stories that have circulated in her hometown of Philadelphia for years.[4]

Researching her ninety-six-year life was an exciting privilege, but time-consuming. Those who remember Marian Anderson as simply a great singer are missing 90 percent of what this trailblazing humanitarian really accomplished.

Readers of this condensed compilation can now more quickly realize, and learn to appreciate, the teachable lessons of Marian Anderson's well-lived long life—possibly in just one or two sittings, stimulating further future study of her from the above sources and the list of books included in the appendix.

It should be noted that from 1925 to 1965, Marian traveled extensively, performing solo concerts throughout the world, but Philadelphia was always in her heart and her true home base. A hallmark of her concerts was always a selection of negro spirituals that she had sung since the age of six in her church's choir.

This timeline is enhanced by internet links such as https://www.vanwyckgazette.com/theater-1/marian-anderson-americas-great-contralto-lscbw and additional internet links herein. Readers are encouraged to investigate all of them by simply clicking on or copying and pasting them into your browser.

In closing, Marian Anderson's God-given talent of vocal genius—given the solo concerts she performed in nine languages, with her ability to speak five of them fluently—and her many more talents that extended beyond her musical prowess, as she displayed skills and interests as a fashion designer, seamstress, dark room photographer, farm gardener, cook, homemaker, furniture upholsterer, international celebrity and diplomat, and lover of children and animals—are some of her many qualities, heretofore not before condensed and presented in one work.

Why not before? Marian Anderson's nephew, James DePreist, sums it up in his loving foreword to her autobiography *My Lord, What a*

Morning: "When I think of those qualities most often associated with Marian Anderson, humility first comes to mind, humility anchored in faith and gratitude for her gifts. Arrogance was inconceivable. My aunt never felt that her successes were hers alone, rather they were primarily God's doing. "My part in it is very small indeed," she would say." (I encourage readers to get this book and take it to heart.)

For someone born into this world so socially disadvantaged, having to overcome obstacles and persecution throughout much of her adult life that are unimaginable today—always with grace and dignity—are inspirational lessons we need to always remember and pass on to our future generations.

Acknowledgments

Researching, compiling, and writing this book was made possible through the inspiration and leading of my personal Lord and Savior, Jesus Christ, who also led and inspired Marian Anderson throughout her life.

I am indebted in major ways to several key sources:

- The excellent political history book about Marian Anderson's accomplishments written in 2009 by Raymond Arsenault: *The Sound of Freedom: Marian Anderson, the Lincoln Memorial, and the Concert that Awakened America*, a must-read for history buffs.

- The definitive original Marian Anderson biography published in 2000 by Allan Keiler, *Marian Anderson: A Singer's Journey*. This book, a fantastic read, is the culmination of Dr. Keiler's lifelong fascination with Marian Anderson. He superbly documented the life of this guarded public figure—who is still revered today. His work has enhanced the history of both American music and the civil rights movement by illuminating the life of Marian Anderson—one of the twentieth century's greatest artists. The preponderance of information in this condensed compilation is drawn from Dr. Keiler's seven years of work. Thank you, and God bless you, Allan!

- The staff at the University of Pennsylvania Library, to which Marian Anderson originally donated her vast personal papers, records, and photographs in 1977, and added to with more donations in 1991 when additional personal papers were donated by James DePriest, Marian Anderson's nephew and sole heir, who is also a Penn Alumnus. Today, this professionally curated and catalogued collection of the Marian Anderson Papers has been digitized and is available for viewing on-line at https://penntoday.upenn.edu/news/newly-digitized-marian-anderson-collection-now-accessible-online. For direct access to the Marian Anderson Collection: https://mariananderson.exhibits.library.upenn.edu/

- An extensive organized listing of 1,344 citations from hundreds of publications including books and newspaper and magazine articles from around the world as of 1981, all logically categorized and indexed. Compiled by Janet L. Sims: *Marian Anderson: An Annotated Bibliography and Discography*. This is an incredibly fine work, though, unfortunately, it has no references beyond 1981.

I want to thank Bill Nicoletti of Going the Distance Films for producing and directing the excellent, award-winning film, *Once in a Hundred Years: The Life And Legacy of Marian Anderson*. Now available on Amazon.com.

I thank, from the bottom of my heart, Jillian Patricia Pirtle, the dedicated and talented CEO of the National Marian Anderson Historic Society and Residence Museum (NMAHS) and apologize for all the times I have bugged her while trying to better understand and help the cause of preserving the memory and legacy of our "Great Lady From Philadelphia."

The NMAHS is an IRS 501(c)(3) tax exempt organization and deserving of your support. Please visit their website here: http://marianandersonhistoricalsociety.weebly.com/

Most of all, I am grateful for my dear wife of forty-seven years, Penny, for her love and support and for allowing me to commandeer our kitchen table with my laptop computer and piles of books, file folders, and papers during the many months of research while compiling this book.

And many thanks for the expert publishing consultants from Xlibris, Dean Summers and Travis Black, for their personal guidance and encouragement—a major factor in the completion of this book.

Chronology

- **1897** – Marian Anderson was born February 27 at 1833 Webster Street, in South Philadelphia, the first of three girls, to Anna Delilah Rucker Anderson and John Berkley Anderson. From a young age Marian's musical talent was apparent and completely nurtured by her parents.

- **1903** – At age six, Marian began performing with the Union Baptist Church junior choir, becoming a member of the senior choir at age thirteen.

- **1905** – Marian made her first public appearance at age eight, when she sang to help her church raise funds. She was billed as the "Baby Contralto." Marian said that one experience of her schoolgirl days which stands out was when she sang on the same platform as Roland Hayes, an internationally acclaimed tenor who later became her friend and mentor.

- **1907** – At age ten, she was chosen to become a member of The People's Choir (predecessor to today's popular public community choirs).

- **1910** – In January, her beloved father, John Berkley Anderson, age 34, died at home, the month after an accidental head injury sustained at work while building the Reading Railroad Train

Terminal in downtown Philadelphia. Marian moved with her mother and two sisters into the home of her father's parents, Benjamin and Isabella Anderson.

- **1912** – Marian graduated from Stanton Grammar School, then postponed entering high school to earn money to help support her family by scrubbing neighborhood steps, delivering laundry, domestic work, etc.

- **1915** – After waiting while all the others in line behind her were waited on, Marian was denied even an application for the Philadelphia Music Academy. When finally told, "We don't take colored here," she left, humiliated and shocked. Later, she entered William Penn High School.

  1915 – She began public solo concert tours, predominately in Philadelphia's black churches, with fellow students of Mary Saunders Patterson, who became her first vocal instructor.

- **1916** – In order to earn more money to help her family, Marian began to travel for concert tours while still in high school, which impeded her academic progress.

- **1918** – She transferred to South Philadelphia High School for Girls, beginning as a twenty-one-year-old freshman.

- **1919** – Dr. Lucy Wilson, Marian's high school principal, introduced her to Giuseppe Boghetti, a leading voice coach. Union Baptist Church members continued to contribute for her voice lessons. (Marian always remembered this kindness and generosity, gratefully paying it forward for the rest of her life.)

- **1920** – Marian successfully auditioned with Giuseppe Boghetti by singing "Deep River," almost bringing him to tears. After one year of funding by Marian's church, Boghetti provided her with one year of free lessons.

- **1921** – She graduated from South Philadelphia High School for Girls.

- **1924** – She became the first black recording artist under contract by RCA Records (originally The Victor Talking Machine Company, predecessor to RCA Victor—today one of the flagship labels of Sony Music Entertainment). She was under a nonexclusive contract with RCA for most of her professional career of more than forty years, producing nearly a hundred recordings ... likely the most by any RCA artist to this day.[4]

1924 – Since they first dated in high school, and after his many attempts to move Marian to marry him, Orpheus "King" Fisher eventually started dating other women and married Ida Gould, a University of Pennsylvania Nursing School graduate. One year later their son, James Fisher, was born. After a few years Orpheus and Ida separated. While they were not divorced until December 1940, James is raised by Ida and her mother, adopting the Gould family name.

1924 – From her modest earnings as a singer, Marian and her family purchased a house at 762 S. Martin Street for $4,000—across from Union Baptist Church—to provide a home for her mother and two sisters. Today this is the site of the Marian Anderson Residence Museum.[1]

1924 – Demoralized by a disappointing first appearance at New York's Town Hall in April, for months Marian did not think about singing as she sorted out conflicts of self-doubt about her future. After much encouragement from friends, in the fall, Marian and Billy King, her accompanist for the past several years, began touring again.

1924 – On December 23, Marian became the first black artist to appear as a soloist with the Philadelphia Philharmonic Society at Philadelphia's Academy of Music.

• **1925** – Marian won first place from among three hundred contestants during a competition at Lewisohn Stadium in New York City sponsored by the New York Philharmonic. As the winner she earned the opportunity to perform a solo concert with the orchestra on August 26, 1925, receiving rave reviews— her first big break. She remained in New York to pursue further studies with Frank La Forge. During that time Arthur Judson, who managed the New York Philharmonic and the Philadelphia Orchestra, became her manager.

• **1928** – Using her own savings, Marian courageously set out on her first of several continual European trips to reduce the impact of racial discrimination on her career and further her training. Destination: London. After several months of intensive training in London, she performed a solo concert at London's Wigmore Hall on June 15—her European debut. Upon returning from Europe, she sang again at the Academy of Music and had her solo concert debut at Carnegie Hall.

• **1929** – She performed solo concert tours in much of the United States. Following a concert in Chicago, she was introduced to two members of the Rosenwald Committee, who suggested that she should submit a grant application to the Rosenwald Foundation.

• **1930** – On June 12 Marian set sail for Europe from New York City after being awarded the first of two six-month study fellowships from the Rosenwald Foundation. Destination: Berlin.

1930 – She continued intensive language and voice training in Germany. Decided, after much consideration, to use five hundred dollars of her own Travelers Checks to finance her concert debut in Berlin at the Bachsaal on October 10. Marian's performance was well received and appreciated by the large audience, with sensational praise from all the critics for several weeks. During this time, Marian was invited to many places, making friends and expanding her network. Male suitors were attracted, but she was not interested. She received and accepted a serious invitation to perform concerts in Scandinavia.

1930 – That summer in Scandinavia, Marian met Finnish pianist Kosti Vehanen, who became her regular accompanist and vocal coach for many years. Through Vehanen she met Jean Sibelius after he had heard her in a concert in Helsinki.

During a meeting at his home, Sibelius, an incredibly famous Finnish composer, and violinist, commented to Marian that he felt that her Helsinki performance had "penetrated the Nordic soul." The two struck up an immediate friendship, which further blossomed into a professional partnership, and for many years Sibelius altered and composed songs for Marian to perform.

1930 – She returned home to Philadelphia in time for a family Christmas on Martin Street.

- **1931** – The Judson Agency finally came through with an extensive concert schedule throughout the United States, concluding with a concert in Atlantic City on May 14. Orpheus Fisher, known to his friends as "King," traveled from Philadelphia, hoping to spend the night with her, but Marian stood him up, instead returning home to be with her mother. Orpheus expressed his disappointment in a personal note to Marian.

1931 – In late May, Marian returned to Berlin. Her increased proficiency with the language and her German lieder performances began to win the hearts of her German fans.

- **1932** – King continued his pursuit of Marian. The hard-economic times from the Depression dried up the Judson Agency's once promising concert schedule. Marian resumed her studies with LaForge, and her youngest sister, Alyse, became increasingly involved with the Roosevelt New Deal–era politics. In June, her sister Ethel married James DePriest in the Anderson home on South Martin Street with the Reverend Charles Tindly officiating.

  1932 – With failing prospects in the United States, Marian set sail in October to return to Sweden for the promise of twenty concerts in Scandinavia.

- **1933** – She performed 142 concerts in eight months in Scandinavia and Europe between September 1933 and April 1934. The extensive publicity enticed the King of Sweden to attend her October 20 concert in Stockholm, as "Marian Fever" spread throughout the Continent. "The Lady from Philadelphia" was declared to be part of "Europe's Musical Royalty."

- **1934** – Marian continued performing solo concerts in France, the United States, Russia, and Austria.

  1934 – During a concert intermission at the Mozarteum in Salzburg, Maestro Arturo Toscanini, Europe's leading music personality, came backstage declaring to Marian, in the presence of others, that "what I heard today, one is privileged to hear only *once in a hundred years.*" This was later heavily promoted by Sol Hurok as part of the "Anderson fairy tale," tremendously enhancing her career.

  1935 – Following a Paris concert, one of the world's leading impresarios, **Sol Hurok,** offered Marian a better contract than she previously had with Arthur Judson. Hurok became her manager for the rest of her performing career. He brought her back to perform in America, booking her for the entire season beginning with her second recital appearance in New York City's Town Hall on December 30, for which she received highly favorable reviews by music critics, especially Howard Taubman of the *New York Times*.

- **1936** – On January 16, Marian again sang at the Academy of Music in Philadelphia—her emotional homecoming. The press was ecstatic. Four days later, on the twentieth, she sang again at Carnegie Hall to a full house with rave reviews. Shortly thereafter, she became one of the few black entertainers ever to be invited to perform at the White House. She brought her mother, Anna, with her to meet President and Mrs. Roosevelt, before returning to Europe in March.

1936 – While still in Europe, Marian received word that her sister Ethel had given birth to her nephew Jimmy on November 21. Marian was ecstatic and could not wait to get home to begin what became a lifetime of doting over him.

- **1937** – She departed Europe for home in January. During this period, the late 1930s, Marian gave about seventy recitals a year throughout the United States. Although by then quite famous, her stature did not completely end the prejudice she confronted as a young black singer touring the United States. She was still denied rooms in many American hotels and was not allowed to eat in many American restaurants.

    Albert Einstein, a champion of racial tolerance, hosted Marian Anderson at his home on many occasions, the first being in 1937 when she was denied accommodations at the Nassau Inn before performing at Princeton University. Marian and Dr. Einstein frequently communicated and occasionally traveled over the years to black colleges and universities when Dr. Einstein was invited as a guest lecturer. On average, Marian visited him at his home in Princeton every year, up until two months before he died in 1955.

- **1938** – Marian began her third year under Hurok Management, which included sixty concerts between the new year and the end of May. Her fourth season of eighty concerts began at Thanksgiving, continuing to the middle of June 1939—one of the longest and most strenuous tours ever undertaken by an American artist, during which she grossed $238,000 (in 2020 dollars, the equivalent of $6 million).[3]

1938 – In late March, Marian appeared at Town Hall in the eighth and final event of the Town Hall endowment series. She had to repeat several encores. On March 31, the *New York Times* writer stated, "Her singing had dignity and simplicity, tenderness and nobility, passion and humanity." Just as Marian always conducted her life both on and off stage.

1938 – In June Marian received her first honorary Doctor of Music degree, from Howard University. Fifty more followed over her lifetime. By this time, Howard University and the NAACP had already joined forces to battle the DAR (Daughters of the American Revolution) … a battle that would be one of the greatest milestones in the struggle for racial equality in America.

- **1939** – The historic Lincoln Memorial Concert took place on Easter Sunday, April 9, and is well documented by the mass media and in books by noted historians. Walter White, the head of the NAACP, was the true architect of this event. The president of Howard University was concerned about a potential Ku Klux Klan disruption. Many threats of violence and safety concerns caused Marian to call Sol Hurok at midnight the night before the concert, wanting to cancel.

    In a nutshell: Following three unsuccessful attempts over two years by Howard University, early in the year, Sol Hurok was also unsuccessful trying to book Constitution Hall for a Washington, DC, concert due to their "white performers only" policy, brought on by Jim Crow laws and Washington, DC's, segregation customs. Constitution Hall was owned by the DAR. Public outrage resulted. Eleanor Roosevelt and several hundred other DAR members resigned in protest. Ultimately, largely due to Eleanor Roosevelt's influence, this led to Marian Anderson's outdoor Easter Sunday solo concert on the steps of the Lincoln Memorial, in front of 75,000 people and millions on national radio.

This was the largest crowd ever at that point on the National Mall. There was a very heavy police presence. Historians now recognize this peaceful protest event as the true beginning of the modern Civil Rights era.

What historians have overlooked is that a bright and impressionable ten-year-old boy named Martin Luther King Jr. was in the audience, carefully listening. Twenty-four years later, in 1963, when he delivered his historic "I have a dream" speech, Dr. King quoted the lyrics from Marian's entire opening song in 1939, "America" (*"My country, 'tis of thee, sweet land of liberty"* … etc.) on those same sacred steps, where he and his dear friend and mentor, Marian, made history again in 1963.[2]

More about this landmark concert is on permanent display at the Smithsonian's National Museum of African American History and Culture in Washington, DC.

1939 – On June 8, Marian was invited back to the White House to perform at a private reception in honor of England's King George VI and Queen Elizabeth.

1939 – On July 2, Marian received the NAACP's prestigious Spingarn Gold Medal, awarded for the highest or noblest achievement by a living African American during the preceding year or years. Presented for the first time by First Lady Eleanor

Roosevelt, the Spingarn Award is an honor carrying more prestige than any other in the black community.

- **1940** – Because of the staggering amount of publicity from her Washington appearance and the increased demand for concerts in all parts of the country, Marian thought the time had come to approach Hurok for a better contract.

  What they agreed to was that Marian would sing no more than fifty to sixty concerts in the States a year, and she would receive two-thirds of the gross for each concert, instead of a fixed fee, the kind of contract, in fact, that Hurok reserved for his most important artists.

  This was to be her last year with Kosti, which ended in the summer of 1940, when Marian gave nearly eighty concerts in the States alone. Following Kosti's return to Scandinavia, Hurok contracted with German-American pianist Franz Rupp to become Marian's permanent accompanist. This partnership lasted until her retirement from the stage in 1965. The first of their concerts that season was in Harrisburg, Pennsylvania.

- **1941** – In March, Marian received the prestigious Philadelphia BOK Award (later renamed The Philadelphia Award) with a $10,000 cash gift from the City of Philadelphia recognizing Marian Anderson as its outstanding citizen.

  As she promised during the event, the following year, Marian used the $10,000 to seed a perpetual endowment fund annually providing Marian Anderson Scholarships for talented young people ranging from several hundred to $1,000 each. (In 2020 dollars this endowment is equivalent to $263,885.)[3].

1941 – Their first season over, in late June and early July, and again in September, Marian and Rupp prepared for their first recording sessions in the studio built by King at Marianna Farm.

- **1942** – Marian's touring during the war included singing for many impromptu audiences of servicemen in hospitals and military establishments across the country. For Marian, concerts for the troops were occasions to lighten the mood and to recall the pleasures of home and family for young men who were about to go to war.

  The chance to talk to servicemen and the unrestrained demonstrations of gratitude from the troops brought out her natural warmth, humor, and unaffected directness, qualities that were less apparent in the formal setting of a concert hall.

  At a Topeka military hospital, she sang for wounded men who could not sit for very long, but they did for forty-five minutes and would not let her go.

  At a camp for black solders near Seattle, she sang for the men as they stood in formation.

  In Sausalito, California, a free concert was arranged at the Marin Shipyards for a few hundred solders and a large number of shipyard workers and civilian visitors and other dignitaries as she christened the USS *Booker T. Washington*, the first of seventeen WWII Liberty cargo ships named after famous African Americans.

  She returned east via Shepherd Field in Texas, thousands of men stood waiting on the field when their plane landed.

1942 – In mid-September Ethel's husband, James DePriest, was gravely ill in Jefferson Hospital with heart disease. At only forty-eight years old, DePriest died on October 7. Ethel and the family were devastated. The burden she now carried of raising a son who was then only six years old intensified Marian's caregiving instincts, which now required planning and emotional support for her sister and nephew.

1942 – On November 2, Marian made her first appearance on *The Bell Telephone Hour*. She became immensely popular with radio audiences, making three or four appearances each season throughout the next decade.

The *Telephone Hour* did not disrupt her schedule of concerts, which continued much as it had before the war, beginning in early October and ending in early May, with trips to the Midwest states in the early winter, and northwest in January and February. Each season, Marian gave as many as four concerts in Carnegie Hall—at the start of the season, in early January, and in the spring—many of which were benefits.

Since 1935 she had performed in 178 cities across the country, singing in all but seven states. Hurok hired Isaac Jofe as her traveling manager to arrange schedules and accommodations and to shield her from any hostility, insult, and humiliation she might meet from hotel staff, from local theatre managers, and in restaurants.

On the road for as many as six or seven months of the year, Marian packed and unpacked over twenty pieces of luggage in every city, including an iron and ironing board, sewing machine, radio, recording machine, hot plate, sleeping bag, and assorted dishes. Some of these things went along to make it possible for her to avoid confrontation; she could boil eggs or soup in her room, for example, when she was not welcome in the hotel dining room. Other items supported her projects for the long months away from home, such as sewing curtains or clothes for the summer.

• **1943** – After months of media squabbling, with the press doing what it could to stir up the old controversy, Marian had already privately decided that she would not let the DAR's refusal to lift its ban on black artists at Constitution Hall prevent her from contributing to the war effort. Finally, the DAR invited her to perform on January 7 at Constitution Hall—to a sold-out, integrated audience—as part of a benefit for the American Red Cross.

The DAR, in a genuine spirit of compromise, accepted the demand that the concert be unsegregated, the first time in its history that it permitted such a concert to be held in the hall.

After the concert, when questioned by the story-hungry press looking to fan the flames for a follow-on story to her 1939 experience, Marian graciously said of the event, "When I finally walked onto the stage of Constitution Hall, I felt no different than I had in other halls. There was no sense of triumph. I felt that it was a beautiful concert hall and I was very happy to sing there."

1943 – Exactly one week before the Constitution Hall concert, Interior Secretary Harold Ickes announced that a special ceremony was to be held in the Department of the Interior's South Building on the evening of January 6, to dedicate Mitchell Jamieson's mural commemorating the now famous historic concert at the Lincoln Memorial in 1939. Many of the key figures of the Washington coalition that had brought together the Lincoln Memorial concert were present.

1943 – In March, King gave up his architectural position in New York to settle permanently on the farm, taking a position as a draftsman with the Barden Corporation, a manufacturer of precision ball bearings for the famous Norden bombsight, which became indispensable to the precision bombing that made possible the shift in air power in Europe from German to Allied hands.

1943 – With King having worked over several years on Marianna Farm and moved from New York to Danbury, marriage was a long time in coming. In December of 1940, King's divorce from Ida Gould had been finalized. On July 17, 1943, following a long courtship, Marian married architect Orpheus "King" Fisher during a quiet ceremony in Bethel Methodist Church near Marianna Farm in Danbury.

There were many happy gatherings of family and friends at Marianna Farm now that King and Marian were finally settled in. The public was not notified about the marriage until a Hurok Agency press release in mid-November while Marian was on tour in the Midwest. At age forty-six, beyond childbearing years, Marian nonetheless remained dedicated to helping children in need.

- **1944** – Due to the rationing of materials for making records during the war, Marian did not return to the recording studio until December. From then until the end of 1947 there were regular sessions in the spring and early summer months, and often late in the year.

- **1945** – Interestingly, Marian Anderson's long-time manager, Sol Hurok, became **Jackie Robinson's** baseball agent. A close friendship between the three for the rest of their lives enabled Jackie to privately learn, through Hurok and Marian, the power of grace and dignity in the face of persecution. Their relationship led filmmaker Bill Nicoletti to proclaim, "Marian Anderson is the Jackie Robinson of the arts."[2]

- **1946** – Soon after the holiday season, doctors discovered a small cyst on her esophagus. King urged Marian to have the operation immediately so that she could be well by spring. No one was sure she would be able to sing after such an operation. Ignoring the possible consequences of not acting quickly, fearful of ill health and possibly even retirement, Marian concentrated on the commitments of a long concert season that lay just ahead. The year ended triumphantly with a cover story in *Time* magazine.

- **1947** – Meanwhile, after the war, Marian became a founding board member of the Chapel of Four Chaplains Memorial Foundation (http://www.fourchaplains.org/), then headquartered at Temple University (located today at the original Philadelphia Navy Yard

Chapel). She served as an active member on the Foundation's board for forty years.

1947 – In the spring during a tour of the West Indies, in the intense heat, Marian's health began to suffer. She returned home completely exhausted, with a sore throat. A month passed, and it grew worse. The doctor thought she had an infection, perhaps from a tropical germ she picked up during the tour. During the summer she had little appetite and lost twenty pounds. Nonetheless, throughout the autumn of 1947 and into spring of 1948, she kept her concert engagements, maintaining a grueling schedule, often with only one day of rest.

1947 – On April 15th Jackie Robinson became the player who shattered racial barriers when he integrated baseball. But before he could swing a bat in the major leagues or even step onto the field, he had to be signed by someone who believed in equality, who believed that it wasn't right for America's sport to be divided by the color of its players' skin. This man was Branch Rickey, an executive of the Brooklyn Dodgers who initiated the "noble experiment" of integration.

Rickey's search for "the right man" officially began in 1943 when the Dodgers' management gave him the go-ahead. It wasn't long after then when Rickey and Hurok discovered a common denominator, in what Sol Hurok had been building and learning from Marian since 1935, that served as a ready-made springboard for Rickey's noble experiment—using Hurok's successes managing Marian Anderson's professional career as a stepping-stone for success in Sol Hurok's new additional role as Jackie Robinson's baseball agent.[4]

• **1948** – Following a series of tests and X-rays, on June 28, Marian checked into the Jewish Hospital in Brooklyn and was operated on the next day to finally remove a cyst from her esophagus. The operation was very intricate and extremely delicate. The least deviation could have permanently injured her vocal cords. Discharging her from the hospital twelve days later, the doctors cautioned her not to sing.

Not until August did the doctors feel she was ready to test her voice. She sent for Rupp, who came at the end of the month. She first sang a little French song that she had never done before, singing it from beginning to end without the slightest difficulty. After that, she knew she was well. On October 13, before an audience of six thousand at Ann Arbor's Hill Auditorium, at no time did she feel unable to go to the end. A month later, in her first Carnegie Hall concert of the season, her three doctors and her nurse came to hear her. Everyone was happy for her.

• **1949** – Successfully recovered from her career-threatening throat surgery and convalescence, she was unshaken in her resolve to continue to perform as she had before. She was, as always, prepared to trust in God. Since she could not alter what God had in store for her, on the practical side, she could at least influence what Hurok was willing to pay her for her work in the years that remained. Before the year's end she instructed her lawyer, Hubert T. Delany, Esq., to inform Hurok that "in light of the experiences of the current season and other relevant considerations," she wanted a new contract. Hurok agreed to an increase from two-thirds to seventy percent of the income from her concerts.

On April 28, four days after her last concert of the season at Carnegie Hall, Marian sailed on the *Queen Elizabeth* for a two-month tour of Europe that would take her to Paris and London, Scandinavia, Switzerland, Belgium, and the Netherlands. The excitement and hospitality that greeted Marian and Rupp, the sold-out concerts with stage seating virtually everywhere, was far greater than she had ever expected.

On May 16 upon their arrival in Helsinki, Kosti intercepted her immediately at the airport. They were to perform at the Messuhalli the following evening. The mood of excitement and celebration was heightened the following afternoon when

Avra Warren, the American ambassador to Finland, with many Finnish and American dignitaries present, presented Marian with the Order of the White Rose during a ceremony at the American embassy—Finland's highest civilian honor in recognition of service to Finnish art and culture.

The Order of the White Rose was presented to Marian for her long years of dedication to the music of Sibelius and Kilpinen. Kosti accompanied Marian that evening for the largest concert of the entire tour. Seven thousand people thronged the Great Hall, with many turned away. People were packed solid—standing room only—up and down the stairway. Upon leaving the hall the happy throng surrounded her car, banging their approval on the fenders and windows.

On June 3, Marian arrived in Zurich from Copenhagen for the second part of the tour. If the concerts in Scandinavia were the high point of the tour, the low point came by the time she reached still war-torn and depressed Belgium for a concert on the fifteenth in Brussels and the seventeenth in Liège. The critics seemed to reflect the same state of mind of Belgium's postwar malaise.

By this time, she was getting tired and looking forward to the European vacation she and King had planned for July and August. They decided to meet in Paris before her final concert in Deauville.

After vacationing in France and then for the rest of August in Sweden with Marian's Scandinavian manager, Helmer Enwall, and his wife, Terese, they returned home to rest and prepare with Rupp for Marian's fifteenth annual American tour beginning with a recital in Carnegie Hall on November 30. These annual American tours in the fall and winter months, concerts in Central America in the spring, a European and then South American tour in the summer—this was now the extended season that continued throughout most of the decade with only occasional variation.

Only the growing criticism of her unyielding middle-of-the-road position on segregated audiences in the South marred the enthusiastic acclaim that greeted her on both continents. *Newsweek*, in a cover story on Marian Anderson in April 1949, had drawn attention to her concert in Montgomery, Alabama, the previous January and praised "her way of touring the South— demanding her vertical theatre seating, yet bowing to regional custom by avoiding hotels exclusively patronized by whites."

This sensible middle-of-the-road compromise position bothered some blacks who were fighting for total desegregation with their unimaginative "it's either my way or the highway" mentality with militant boycotting and protest tactics. The local president of the Richmond chapter of the NAACP wrote to Marian explaining their position and informing her they planned "to urge all of our members and other freedom-loving citizens to refrain from attending your concert or any other affair unless segregated conditions are not to prevail." Marian undoubtedly discussed the matter with Hurok; publicly she remained silent. Walter White, the head of the NAACP, lent his support to the Richmond branch, urging Hurok to act in accordance with the Richmond branch's efforts. On January 12, White received word of Hurok and Marian's position:

> "We feel strongly that under the circumstances it would be unwise to make an issue of the segregation at this time, and indeed, unfair to Miss Anderson. We feel, and many people share our view, that Miss Anderson's policy in the years past has resulted in a vast improvement in the relations between Negro and white in the Southern states and has brought the problem of segregation closer to a real solution than would have been the case if she had followed more militant tactics."

The powerful gift of Marian Anderson's God-given talent and genius was obviously neither understood nor appreciated by anxious militants. Indeed, many believed that as the best known and best loved role model for Negro youth, she should not surrender to segregation lest she destroy some of the love young people had for her.

• **1950** – The first leg of her fifteenth season after Carnegie Hall would take her from the States to Europe and then to South America before its conclusion ten months later. Before leaving for Europe, Marian and King agreed it was time to "downsize," listing their large home for sale with the fifty acres on which it stood. King was already busy with plans to design and help to build a new, smaller, more private one-story three-bedroom rancher across the road that would make it more difficult for family and friends to visit so easily.

The second leg of her tour in Europe included Paris, London, Berlin, Munich, Zurich, and Geneva—a dozen European concerts in all. The concerts in Europe were a series of triumphs. Overall, the audiences were often smaller than they had been before the war, yet the enthusiasm of audiences and critics alike made for rhapsodic receptions. The concerts in Germany were the most gratifying for both. Until then, neither had performed together before German-speaking audiences, and both were returning to the earlier days of their musical studies, Marian in Berlin and Rupp at the Munich Conservancy.

In Berlin, a mixed Allied and German audience filled the Titania Palast, with half the tickets given to students. Major General Maxwell Taylor, the commander of allied troops in Berlin, flew in from Frankfurt to attend the performance. There was tremendous applause throughout the program, with the most coming after the last spiritual, "O What a Beautiful City!" The critic of the *Neue Zeitung* epitomized the press reception at both concerts, dwelling particularly on the "astonishing empathy and adaptability with which Anderson made the specifically German emotional world of the Schubert lied her own." Marian had not sung in Germany since the day she stood before a small circle of friends and well-wishers in the Psychological Institute in

Berlin nearly twenty years before, trying out for the first time in public the Brahms *Vier ernste Gesänge*. Now a German audience was welcoming her home artistically. As the *Neue Zeitung* critic wrote, "[In] critical places one is surprised by a wonderfully accomplished phrase or even a single tone in which her soul seems to open. From such moments the whole song achieves a new illumination. Her natural expressiveness imparts to songs like 'Der Erlkönig' and 'Der Tod und das Mädchen' a deeply moving dramatic power, while [in] others like 'Liebesbotschaft,' the charm of her delivery is spellbinding," The European tour ended in Genoa on July 21.

From there, Marian sailed for South America for a tour of twenty concerts that would extend into the second week of September. As during the previous summer, King joined Marian for part of the South American tour, meeting up with her in Rio, prepared to fly home should their property be sold.

- **1952** – Marian listened to the voices of the South. In the last weeks of January, she took her first stand against segregation when singing before unsegregated audiences in Jacksonville and Miami, Florida, for the first time in the history of the state. In Jacksonville, several hundred dissatisfied whites demanded a refund, while in Miami two days later, she was given a parade and a hero's welcome. The Miami concert had the largest police protection ever given an artist. There were no incidents. Cautiously and at her own pace, Marian was changing with the times, and the times were changing *because* of her. In April, a few months after the Florida concerts, Marian sang again at the Lincoln Memorial during the public funeral service for Harold Ickes, closing the circle begun thirteen years earlier.

- **1953** – Early in the year, Marian and Rupp were invited to give a series of concerts in Japan by NHK, the Japanese Broadcasting Company. Their host, Mr. Tetsuro Furukaki, president of NHK, and his representatives greeted them at the Tokyo airport with a huge crowd of people looking on and then took them to their hotel and a press conference, followed by an exquisite traditional Japanese dinner arranged for them by Mr. Furukaki. The tour was to begin at the end of April and continue until the beginning of June. (Before leaving for Japan, as part of an American University concert series, on March 14, Marian again sang to an unsegregated audience in Constitution Hall.)

Marian and Rupp were among the first Western artists to appear in Japan during the postwar period. It was Marian's introduction to the people of Asia, a part of the world that would increasingly become the center of America's foreign policy interests throughout the decade. During the tour they performed ten concerts, including a broadcast and one appearance with the Tokyo Symphony Orchestra. They also performed concerts in Osaka, Nagoya, and Hiroshima. The highlight for Marian was her private audience with Empress Nagako and two of her children, Prince Yoshi and Princess Suga, at the Imperial Palace. It was the first time in its 2,600-year history that a Negro guest had performed for the Imperial Court.

Before leaving Japan, on May 25, she was asked by officials at the American Embassy if it would be possible for her to sing for the troops in Korea. On the morning of May 27, Marian, Rupp, and Jofe, dressed in full army fatigues, left from the Army base in Tokyo for Tague, Korea in a C-119 transport—the Army's "flying boxcar"—with a hundred solders. From there, they boarded a train for Pusan to perform an open-air concert for a huge crowd that had come from long distances in the pouring rain, which was so intense that Marian asked for the concert to be postponed until the following day because of the weather. During the next few days, she sang on improvised stages, in hospital corridors, often to standing audiences huddled together, swaying back and forth.

On May 29, after performing at a Korean hospital, they were taken by helicopter to a UN Danish hospital ship. On final approach to the ship close up, she saw the devastations of war—bombed and burned Korean homes and buildings. Aboard the ship, Marian sang to wounded soldiers receiving blood transfusions. Among the patients she comforted were wounded Turks who had just arrived. At the twenty-first Evacuation Hospital later that day one soldier told her: "I have been here for ten months, Miss Anderson, and after what I heard I can last another ten months."

Before departing from Korea, she told a newspaper interviewer that this part of her tour filled her with tremendous satisfaction and gratitude. In Japan she had been kept away from unpleasantness, but her four days in Korea, with the fighting still going on, brought her face to face with the horrible realities of war. She was shaken by what she saw, but the experience gave her a sense of fulfillment and additional strength that she sorely needed to face any of the segregation issues back in the Southern states. On the first of June, Marian, Rupp, and Jofe returned to Tokyo and continued home via Hawaii following three concerts in Honolulu.

With only three months before a ten-week tour of England and Scotland, Marian threw herself into getting the new house King had built comfortable and properly furnished to turn it into a cozy home for King and herself. By summer's end Marian and King's small circle of close friends and family could be found relaxing around the pool or preparing an outdoor barbecue. The creation of his "dream house" provided King with a much-needed feeling of pride and a new sense of ownership. For her part, although not willing to make any plans toward retirement, Marian, at least during the summer months, became the homemaker King had always hoped for. Others saw their marriage blossom with new respect for each other.

- **1954** – Of all her awards and honors, none meant more to her than the opening of the Marian Anderson Recreation Center, a $700,000 facility at Seventeenth and Fitzwater Streets in South Philadelphia, only two blocks from her house on Martin Street, where she lived most of her early life and where her mother and family still resided. Marian's love and concern for the well-being of her neighborhood's children motivated her to quietly fund much of the construction. At the dedication ceremonies in July, the mayor of Philadelphia, Joseph S. Clark, spoke of the center as the embodiment of a principle "aimed at ending the erosion of human resources, which is a disturbingly prominent feature of present day big-city life."

- **1955** – Since its founding, New York's venerable Metropolitan Opera had gone seventy-two years without a single African American soloist. On January 7, Marian broke the race barrier when she sang the role of the sorceress, Ulrica, in Giuseppe Verdi's *A Masked Ball*. On opening night, the audience gave a thunderous ovation for five minutes before Marian could sing a note, forever changing the face of opera for black singers.

1955 – Near the end of March, Marian flew to Rome on her way to Israel for a series of concerts during April. She wanted to visit the land that provided the source and inspiration for many of the spirituals she sang.

In Rome she felt the beginnings of a virus, but the crowed flight to Israel during Passover took her mind off it. There was a big turnout at Lod airport with representatives from the American embassy and the Israel Philharmonic and an unexpected happy visit with Mrs. Roosevelt, who was flying out a few hours later. By the time Marian saw a doctor the next morning, the virus had worsened, and the first rehearsal and concert had to be postponed. After the rehearsal, a specialist recommended inhalations of streptomycin and penicillin to relieve congestion in her trachea.

On April 2, after a second cancellation, Marian made her first appearance with the Israel Philharmonic. During this time, the German language was boycotted in Israel. Therefore, for each of her recitals Marian chose to learn the entire text of her part in Hebrew, in order to sing her German lieder part in Hebrew for the Israeli audiences. The memory of her dear grandfather, Benjamin, a professed "black Jew," was no doubt on her mind. As always, she accomplished this linguistic feat with extraordinary precision and naturalness. The audience was moved by her desire to communicate with them, which astonished the critics. As one of them put it "we should mention as well with appreciation Brahms' Rhapsody, which was sung in perfect and articulate Hebrew. Because the translation was hard to grasp, the complex words rang out from the great singer more naturally than their content was understood by the audience."

The tour turned into one of the most grueling that Hurok had ever arranged. Because of the small size of Tel Aviv's Edison Hall, where the Israel Philharmonic regularly performed, thirteen appearances were required for each subscription concert to accommodate the public. During the latter part of April when Marian would be joined by Rupp, two additional concerts were in Tel Aviv, plus Haifa—sixteen appearances in less than three weeks. Fortunately, her voice had recovered., Helping to celebrate Passover and singing at various kibbutzes in the region of the Sea of Galilee, the Dead Sea, and the River Jordan, Marian experienced the biblical and historic sites she visited as a pilgrim to the land she had sung about all her life. She could see in Israel the geographic places that represented the reality of her background and traditions, and they stirred her deeply.

For the Israelis, who had great sympathy with the plight of blacks in America, Marian Anderson's visit had a special appeal that was not shared by any of the other great artists who had come to Israel to perform. She was inspirational to all segments of Israeli society.

At the end of her stay in Israel, impressed by the musical talent of the young people, and wanting to create a bond with the people of Israel, especially its youth, that would last beyond her brief visit, Marian contributed part of her fee to establish an annual scholarship to be awarded each year to several gifted singers.

1955 – Once back home, with Hurok's urging and her great reluctance, beginning in the fall over the course of several months, Marian began the task of collaborating with Howard Taubman, the *New York Times* music writer, who was now her neighbor in Danbury, to write her autobiography. Agonizing for her and arduous for Taubman, it was necessary for them to resort to using a tape recorder. He would prepare in advance a list of topics and questions for Marian. Taubman found her unable to be frank about the difficulties of her childhood or to talk freely about the prejudice and discrimination she faced. Whenever a subject arose that gave her any discomfort where she might have to criticize someone or a situation—including the Lincoln Memorial concert, which she did not want to discuss at all—she more often than not turned the tape recorder off before she was willing to go on. More than once, in the face of her inability to be frank, Taubman threatened to abandon the project.

Once Taubman finished the book, Marian read a draft of the manuscript. She disliked it and among other things wanted all mention of the Lincoln Memorial concert removed. Uncertain about how to proceed, she asked a respected close friend and another neighbor, Rex Stout, a novelist, to read the draft. He told her she was being unreasonable and that Taubman had done a brilliant job.

1955 – The Robin Hood Dell in Philadelphia's beautiful Fairmount Park, originally built in 1929 with plain bench seating, is the summer home of the Philadelphia Orchestra. After twenty-six years it was in serious need of upgrading. Marian quietly and anonymously donated $1 million for the Dell's upgrade. The lead contractor for the project, John B. Kelly, Inc, no doubt recognized the importance of Marian's contribution, as well as his daughter's, Grace Kelly. Soon thereafter, Princess Grace of

Monaco and Marian were known to be very friendly. (Today, in 2020 dollars, this $1 million is equivalent to $12.8 million.)[3,4]

1955 – The honors that came this year included the Swedish government's Litteris et Artibus award, presented to Marian by King Gustav of Sweden during her tour of Scandinavia, and an honorary degree from Dickinson University.

• **1956** – For Marian, Rex Stout was a voice of wisdom and authority. He finally convinced her to allow her autobiography to be published. Picked up by the Viking Press, the book, *My Lord, What a Morning*, came out during the summer and became a bestseller.

• **1957** – During the 1950s, Marian Anderson was becoming one of the most admired and dependable black celebrities in government circles—a black woman of extraordinary accomplishments who was loyal, patriotic, and reluctant to criticize publicly the treatment of blacks. Official Washington recognition of Marian came during the first month of the new year, when she sang the national anthem at inauguration ceremonies for President Eisenhower's second term. Since one of the most dramatic and symbolically important breakthroughs for blacks during his first term was Marian's Metropolitan Opera debut, the Eisenhower administration wanted to keep her accomplishment before the public. Already under way, in fact, were State Department plans for her to act as a goodwill ambassador as part of its gradually expanding program of international cultural exchange.

Anxious to combat the Soviet propaganda—that democratic ideals in the United States counted for little when it came to minorities—State Department officials were eager to include black artists in their plans. The American National Arts Foundation had earlier considered sending Marian Anderson and Leontyne Price to the Soviet Union as part of an American–Soviet cultural exchange, which never materialized. For their part, in 1955 the Soviet Union had already sent to the United States Emil Gilels and David Oistrakh, whose debuts were among the most sensational musical and political events of the decade. It was not Hurok but Columbia Artists Management that presented them to the American public.

When Hurok was ready in 1956 to engage in his own cultural exchange mission with the Soviet Union, he gave no thought to Marian Anderson. For Hurok, Marian Anderson, now in the last decade of her career, was no longer a useful player in the high-stakes cultural competition the Soviets had initiated. Shrewd as ever, Hurok countered by sending two of his young popular artists in their artistic prime: Isaac Stern and Jan Peerce.

The State Department thought differently, aware of the impact Marian's Met debut was having abroad—especially in Asian countries. Flush with new funding to expand cultural exchanges, they engaged the American National Theatre and Academy (ANTA), which had been sending artists abroad since the 1940s, as a contractor and adviser to the State Department's U.S. Information Agency (USIA) to help organize cultural exchanges. ANTA would help the State Department considerably expand its cultural exchange activities to Asia and Africa.

While Hurok was planning carefully for the day when he could bring the Soviet Moiseyev dancers and the Bolshoi Ballet to America, the USIA and ANTA were putting together plans to send Marian on the most ambitious and extended tour of Southeast Asian countries ever undertaken by an American artist.

1957 – Beginning in the last week of September, ANTA and the USIA arranged for Marian to give twenty-six concerts, along with speaking engagements and press conferences, for nine weeks (through November 30), in twelve Asian countries. She officially represented the United States as a special envoy/goodwill ambassador. Seoul and Pusan would be the first stops. Formosa, Hong Kong, and Manila would follow in early October, with concerts in Saigon, Phnom-Penh (Cambodia), Rangoon,

Bangkok, Singapore, and Kuala Lumpur during the remaining weeks of October.

In November, Marian traveled to Ceylon (Colombo and Kandy) and then India (Madras, Bombay, New Delhi, and Calcutta). Engagements in Pakistan (Dacca, Lahore, and Karachi) brought the tour to an end. For some years, Marian had refused to sing more than fifty concerts per season. But her love for her country prevailed. Having turned sixty that year with her voice naturally starting to get tired, she was asked to sing nearly thirty concerts in two months' time.

Planning a "See It Now" television program, a full CBS camera crew of technicians carrying fifteen hundred pounds of equipment was sent along with Edward R. Murrow, the leading broadcast journalist of the day, to record Marian's historic feat. The program was aired on the national TV show *See It Now* upon their arrival home in December. That show, narrated by Murrow and entitled "The Lady from Philadelphia," can still be viewed today by clicking on to this Internet link: https://www.youtube.com/watch?v=6af3IpB9_Ho.

A historical note: In May 1954 following the landmark *Brown* v. *Board of Education* decision of the Supreme Court, the Eisenhower administration was criticized by blacks because of his cautious attitude toward civil rights, especially his unwillingness to act against state-imposed segregation. On September 4, 1957, the issue of school desegregation erupted in the South with ugly force when Governor Orval Faubus of Arkansas ordered the national guard to prevent nine black students from attending Little Rock High School. For three weeks the crisis mounted. When Faubus finally withdrew the national guard personnel on September 23, leaving the students to face an angry mob of several thousand that surrounded the school, President Eisenhower sent federal troops to Little Rock the next morning. That evening in Seoul, Marian and Rupp were scheduled to give the first concert of the tour. Thereafter on the tour, in interviews and press conferences, the reporters and interviewers continually tried hard to bait her.

The CBS camera crew recorded very little of what she told interviewers in Asia, although she did recall some of what she said to an interviewer back in the States a few months after the tour: "We told them that it [the trouble in Little Rock] was an unfortunate thing, and that we were sorry it happened. We felt very grieved about it. We didn't go into any long discussion. This was neither the time, nor the place for it, and we were not sufficiently acquainted with the developments. We were there because we believe in America and if you don't believe in a thing, you shouldn't try to represent it."

Unfortunately, her only comment preserved in the "See It Now" broadcast was taken from a press conference in Rangoon. When one of the reporters asked her, "Would you like to sing for Governor Faubus in Little Rock?" she answered without hesitation: "If it could help at all, I should be very delighted to. If Governor Faubus would be in the frame of mind to accept it for what it is, for what he could get from it, I should be very delighted to do it." What she wanted to convey was that her singing, as a gift not altogether of her own doing, was bound up inextricably with her love for others and her faith. Like one's faith, she was unwilling to deny the gift of her singing to anyone ready to benefit from it.

As Marian came to realize, this nonmusical or extramusical part of the tour, its general or larger significance, overshadowed the concerts in many places. Even more than usual, the spirituals had the most profound effect on the Asian audiences. "In every case these old songs, so full of sorrow for a present life, and full of hope for a future one, touched the hearts of the listeners," she explained. "When I try to think of why the spirituals have this power to erase all barriers and all boundaries, it seems to me probable that it arises from this religious origin and their expression of a religious hope."

On tour they performed in multiple types of venues, all of which were virtually sold out. In Hong Kong, for instance, they sang in a football (soccer) stadium with amplifiers. The stadium held eight thousand people, while many others filled the windows and balconies of the high modern buildings behind it. In some cases—in Delhi, for example—the audience was made up of a small and educated elite who had a great hunger for Western music and artists. At many concerts, important dignitaries and heads of state were prominent.

At Assumption College in Bangkok, the king of Thailand, who sat in a specially raised platform in a roped-off area of the theater, came down from the royal dais to shake hands with Marian and to exchange a few words of greeting, one of the few times in Thailand's entire history that the king rose to greet a visitor. Taken completely by surprise, the audience watched in awe and amazement as the king extended his hand and expressed his delight in Marian's appearance in Thailand.

In India, Prime Minister Nehru and his daughter Indira Gandhi sat as part of the audience in New Delhi; after the concert, Marian was entertained by Nehru in his home, where they discussed the great problems facing his country.

In Rangoon, Premier U Nu came personally to greet her backstage after the concert, saying: "Your performance tonight is a rare combination of good voice, good technique, and very good dramatic acting." He went on to say, "The beauty and charm of your music are manifested in your dazzling eyes and childlike lips."

In Kuala Lumpur, on the very day on which the Malaysian flag was raised in the United Nations to celebrate the new nation, Marian, holding fast to the Malay words in her hands lest she forget them, sang the new national anthem in the language of her audience before the concert.

In New Delhi she broke precedent again. Although no visiting dignitary from any foreign nation had ever been invited to speak at the Gandhi memorial, she was granted permission to lay a wreath there. Leading a throng of several thousand people, she was movingly introduced by the mayor of Old Delhi. Marian spoke very little, preferring to sing "Lead, Kindly Light," which she knew was a favorite of Gandhi. Interestingly, two years later, in 1959, Dr. Martin Luther King Jr. and his family followed Marian's visit to the Gandhi Memorial. Dr. King admired Gandhi greatly and practiced his teachings.

• **1958** – The world saw nothing of the emotional cost of the Asian tour on Marian. The recognition it gained her brought a new round of numerous honors that continued throughout the year. Since at least March the Eisenhower administration had included Marian Anderson on a short list of proposed U.S. delegates to the thirteenth session of the United Nations, with Marian as one of five alternate delegates. Worldwide sentiment over her Asian tour had been so positive that the administration wanted to keep Marian Anderson before the public eye. Initially, she declined the offer to serve, feeling inadequate by temperament and knowledge to assume such a role so at odds with the world of singing.

Finally, she turned to Mrs. Roosevelt for advice. By the time Secretary of State Dulles phoned her, in early May, she had changed her mind. On July 23, her name together with the names of nine other appointees were sent to the Senate for confirmation. A few days later the official announcement came that Marian Anderson would be part of the thirteenth United Nations delegation. Having accepted the appointment, she was prepared to face whatever she would be asked to do with undivided seriousness. She canceled all her concert dates and lecture appearances until the new year, planning to stay at her New York apartment with King for the duration of the session.

In view of the success of the Asian tour, and her desire to do work dealing with human rights and race relations, she was assigned to the Trusteeship Council, the committee dealing with all matters relating to the status and well-being of the trust territories. Most of the eleven territories were in the last stages of achieving self-governance since the days of colonial rule (more than half were in Central Africa; the others were island nations in the southwestern Pacific). Few of the new delegates appointed by non-administering UN members were experts in territorial administration. Often delegates acquired familiarity with territorial issues when they participated in missions to the trust territories. Marian, like the other new delegates, would be asked simply to carry out the instructions from her government. The record shows that she served the peoples in the trust territories and the United States diligently and with distinction. The UN session ended on December 13, in time for Marian and King to spend the holidays with their family at Marianna.

- **1959** – In mid-January Marian began her twenty-fourth season under Hurok management. For her Carnegie Hall appearance in March, an event which she always considered the artistic measuring rod for each season, at the age of sixty-two, compounded by the time away from the stage during her UN service, she found it difficult to get started again. For the first time, the critics noticed that "the years have taken the toll of her vocal resources."

  During the spring, *Ebony* magazine, as part of its preparation for the article "Should Marian Anderson Retire?" gathered a sampling of what various critics had reported and decided to approach Marian directly. In Mason City, Iowa, where Marian was giving a concert, a reporter from the magazine asked how she felt about what the critics had been saying about her voice. "The critics," she answered with unruffled calm, "as in all professions must be honest about their feelings whatever they may be— flattering or not. One should always write the truth as one sees it and no one else should influence one." As for retirement, she would decide when the time came to retire, not the critics: "We have thought about retirement, yes, and in that same direction we shall make our decision on retirement on the strength of our own thinking."

The critics surveyed in the *Ebony* article were torn between what their ears told them and their belief in the moral and humanitarian significance of Marian Anderson's presence before the public. Indeed, more than one suggested that given the recent success of her trip to the Far East and her work as a delegate to the United Nations, she could continue as an effective and inspiring symbol of achievement in any number of ways away from the concert platform. Marian expressed, in her direct and eloquent way, the artistic dilemma that all serious artists face as they ponder the question of retirement: "It is impossible to make music like a faucet. It is something in the heart and soul. As long as they move, the music is there. Whether you can bring it forward is something else."

The subject of retirement presented financial concerns as well. Neither she nor King was systematic about investments. Rupp was—which she enjoyed teasing him about. In truth, she envied Rupp's lifelong concern with a financially secure retirement. Marian was still supporting her mother and two sisters. Their needs, in fact, could extend well into the years when she and King were themselves retired. If thoughts of this kind were on Marian's mind when the *Ebony* article appeared, in the early days of June 1960, they must have seemed more relevant than ever, for it was then that she learned of her mother's illness.

Mrs. Anderson had always enjoyed relatively good health. She was now eighty-six years old, somewhat frail yet far from bedridden and suffering intermittently from fluctuations of blood pressure and loss of appetite, symptoms that during the spring had grown serious enough to require both a day and night nurse over a period of many weeks. She was well cared for at home, but Marian was concerned enough to spend a good part of the summer in Philadelphia, taking her old room on Martin Street so that she could look after her mother. "It was a real joy to wait on Mother" she wrote to the Rupps in August when she got back to Marianna Farm.

By the end of the summer, with her mother's health restored, Marian once again enjoyed the serene beauty of the farm, and she felt ready for the start of the new season. Her mother's swift recovery had done wonders for her spirits. So did the zeal with which her European agents beckoned. Plans for a European tour the following season were nearly concluded, and after repeated disappointments, the possibility of an Australian tour now seemed more likely for the summer of 1962.

- **1960** – This was now her twenty-fifth season under Hurok management, and the European tour ran its course through a continual series of concerts, awards and public appearances.

- **1961** – Fast-forward to January 20, 1961. John F. Kennedy had invited Marian Anderson to sing the national anthem during his presidential inauguration ceremony. A few minutes past noon, in weather that old-time political observers said was the worst of any Inauguration Day for any president since Taft in 1913, Marian sang the "Star-Spangled Banner." A few days later at New York's Waldorf-Astoria, she joined fellow artists in a tribute to Sol Hurok, who was being honored by the American-Israel Cultural Foundation for distinguished service in the cause of cultural exchange.

At the end of January, Marian found another reason for satisfaction, this time in a younger colleague's success. Leontyne Price had heard Marian sing in Jackson, Mississippi, when she was nine, an experience that made an indelible impression on her. In 1947, only twenty years old and in her second year of college, she entered the Marian Anderson Competition, traveling to Philadelphia for auditions along with Lenora Lafayette, another scholarship applicant. Feeling that Price showed promise but was not as far along as the other contestants, the judges did not award her a scholarship. Two years later, she entered the Juilliard School of Music. From the time she was invited to sing the role of Bess in the 1952 New York revival of Gershwin's opera, her success was assured.

On January 27, 1961, having already sung in the San Francisco Opera and the Vienna Staatsoper, Leontyne Price made her New York Metropolitan debut as Leonora in Verdi's *Il trovatore*, earning an ovation that lasted over forty minutes—the longest such demonstration ever given in the house—galvanizing the public's attention, thus completing a process of change initiated by Marian six years earlier. In a letter to Marian some weeks after her Met debut, Price wrote "Now I write to thank you from the bottom of my heart. Your name belongs with my Mama and Daddy in spirit and what it contributed to my peace of mind and sense of direction on the night of my debut. God bless you and keep you. You are still my Beacon Light. Straight Ahead!!"

Marian's season ended in April with concerts at Dartmouth College and Concord, New Hampshire. Marian wanted to stay close to home during the summer to be near her mother, whose health had worsened, and to work with Rupp on the coming season which included a European tour in October. But she had agreed to participate in a conference on international peace in the Soviet Union in May and later in the summer to sing at a Casals Festival in San Juan.

No doubt, Marian was asked to participate in "the second Dartmouth conference," held in the Soviet Union in Crimea by the Black Sea, on the basis of her contribution to world understanding and her ability to build bridges between people of different cultures. When the topic of the conference turned to education, Marian spoke: "Education should begin in infancy. You must realize at what an early age a child shows his intention. This is a period to set a pattern by which the child lives his life. The toys I have in mind do not embrace the pistols, the guns, the all kinds of things that could bring sorrow and pain to a playmate. Whatever you teach your child will eventually come out in his makeup."

Less than two weeks after her return from the Soviet Union conference, Marian left for San Juan where she was scheduled to make two appearances at the Casals Festival, on June 14 and 16. Unlike the Crimea conference, where mutual understanding had to be established quickly by participants from different cultures and with different ideologies, the Casals Festival was an annual gathering of musicians who shared a common artistic philosophy. Marian brought her nephew, Jimmy, to San Juan with her as a graduation present and to share with him the unique atmosphere surrounding Casals and the festival musicians.

That summer marked the end of his college years. Jimmy had graduated in 1958 from the Wharton School of the University of Pennsylvania majoring in economics, originally intending to be a lawyer, but by the end of his four years at Wharton he had given up the idea, turning to music as a possible profession. After Wharton, Jimmy entered the University of Pennsylvania's Annenberg School for Communications, thinking he would write music for movies. While at Annenberg, he took courses in theory, harmony, and orchestration at the Philadelphia Conservatory of Music as he studied composition.

In the summer of 1960, his formal education at an end, he was becoming more seriously drawn to the classical repertory, music his Aunt Marian had always shared with him. The friendly and intense atmosphere of music making made a strong impression on Jimmy. He recalled in later years the particular affection and esteem which the musicians, especially Casals, showed his Aunt Marian.

1961 - In October, as she approached the age of sixty-five, Marian left for a two-month tour of Europe, with concerts in London, Paris, and the capitals of Scandinavia. This was the beginning leg of a long season that would include her first tour of Australia and New Zealand in May and June of the following year, after concerts in America. In Scandinavia there was a warm appreciation for her singing of Sibelius and Kilpinen with good critical reviews. However, the absence of Kosti, who had died a few years earlier, saddened her. London was, as usual, cool, emphasizing her vocal problems with more gusto than her musical insights. Paris proved to be the high point of the tour, with the kind of response that for Marian was the highest form of praise.

Before she returned home in early December, there were already plans afoot that would take her back to Europe for Christmas. The West Berlin TV Station, *Sender Freies*, was preparing a Christmas program aimed specifically at the East Berlin audience, now on the other side of the recently built Berlin Wall. Several countries, including the United States, were being asked to contribute their talent. As Edward R. Murrow, then USIA chief, explained to Hurok: "The United States Government is greatly concerned about the welfare of the German population on both sides of 'the Wall' and an interdepartmental decision—at the highest level—has been made to contribute to the success of this program."

The Berlin TV station had specifically asked for the services of Marian Anderson, stating that she was recognized the world over not only as an outstanding singer "but as a person of great dignity, human compassion and sincerity which blends perfectly with the overall theme of the program." Marian and Hurok were informed that the rehearsal and filming of the program was scheduled for December 25. Although this meant that Marian would not be home for Christmas, she was excited to participate.

For her, the invitation had larger connotations. It was a way of aligning herself with the new administration's policy of bringing about greater world understanding and peace. In November she had her first such opportunity under the new administration, when she became a founding member of the Freedom from Hunger Foundation formed by President Kennedy to attract public support and private contributions to aid projects combating hunger in the third world. As a member of the foundation, she felt she was fulfilling a promise she had made to herself since her work in the United Nations. Moreover, she was as much a fan of the new president as anyone. Inspired by his sense of mission, she wanted to do her part.

When Marian and Rupp arrived in West Berlin on the morning of December 23, Dr. Lungh, the director of the radio and TV station, greeted her warmly but expressed surprise that they had chosen to arrive on the day of the performance. They were both stunned, not to mention exhausted by the long trip. There were apologies for the mix-up; the film was to be shown on Christmas Day, but taped two days earlier, and there was only time for forty-five minutes of rest for Marian before she had to tape her segment of the program. The show was broadcast in West Berlin and much of Western Europe, Marian's part consisting of two spirituals and the Lord's Prayer. Marian privately thought the whole affair was mismanaged and was unhappy when she learned that her private view had reached the State Department when they arrived home.

- **1962** – For both Marian and King, the new year began badly and grew steadily worse. On January 31, King was admitted to Danbury Hospital, where tests showed he had diabetes. The news hit him hard. Although for years he had suffered from sinus problems and mild high blood pressure, he had always enjoyed relatively good health. Now in his sixties, he was remarkably vigorous and active, working outdoors on the farm, doing carpentry work, and riding and swimming regularly.

    After only a week in the hospital, King was back at the farm in the first week of February. Thoughts of advancing age and of being less active began to affect his spirits. He was depressed not only about his health but about the start of Marian's new season beginning the following week, and the resulting separation. Appearances in Canada and the West Coast would keep her away from Marianna for most of February and March.

    In conjunction with a concert in the State Department Auditorium in Washington on March 22, part of a series sponsored by the president's cabinet, with Mrs. Kennedy as honorary chairperson, Marian looked forward to the chance to speak with the president. He was unable to attend the concert, however. Disappointed, she asked for a private meeting with him.

Ordinarily, Marian's natural modesty would have held her back from such a request, but her admiration for the president, for his idealism and sense of commitment, encouraged her to act. At a time when she feared her moderation and respect for compromise would be interpreted as passivity, especially by the younger generation, she was looking for an appropriate occasion to express to Kennedy her commitment to the civil rights struggle. More than anything, she dreaded being thought of as no longer relevant to it. Although Kennedy as a rule did not meet with the artists sponsored by the president's cabinet, he agreed to meet with Marian during the afternoon before the concert. She gave him her latest recording of spirituals and received from him a reproduction of the Inauguration emblem.

Most important, the Washington events brought Marian back closer to home. Her schedule finally allowed her some weeks to be with King. In early April, King suffered a slight stroke and had to be hospitalized. Fortunately, the damage was minimal. The doctors were encouraged by his rapid progress, and on the seventeenth he was released from the hospital, overjoyed at his rapid recovery but once again dreading the moment in early May when Marian would have to leave for concerts abroad.

Marian's tour of Australia and New Zealand was the fulfillment of a promise made fifteen years before, when plans for a tour there had to be abandoned because of her throat illness and surgery. Her growing prestige internationally in the intervening years added to the excitement and anticipation felt among concert managers "down under," encouraging Hurok to arrange a long and demanding tour that would last well over a month, from the last week of May until the end of June.

Fifteen appearances were scheduled with concerts in Sydney, Brisbane, Melbourne, and Adelaide. The New Zealand part of the tour included appearances in Auckland and Wellington.

The four concerts in Sidney within a single week required that Marian and Rupp prepare four different programs, adding to the strain of the tour.

To the people and press alike, Marian's tour was akin to a royal visit. "An interview with Marian Anderson," said one Melbourne writer in the *Daily Telegraph*, "is like an audience with a Crowned Head—in fact it'd be easy to imagine her as 'Empress of America,' if there were such an appointment."

All the concerts were sold out, with huge crowds waiting for a glimpse of her as she left the theatre. The critics were more ambivalent; they had been prepared to hear a singer of legendary status rather than one already sixty-five years old and nearing retirement. She received mixed reviews, with some not hiding their disappointment. A critic in Brisbane offered praise for her "unerring sense of style and instinctive feeling for drama."

Then during the first week of June, traveling from Brisbane to Melbourne, Marian developed a cold that grew progressively worse. The next day, she was unable to sing a note during a morning rehearsal. She saw a doctor in the afternoon, who prescribed antibiotic capsules. The concert that night in the Melbourne Town Hall proved "a terrible strain." So did the news from home. Full of news about the farm and animals, King could not hide his loneliness and depression.

By the time she reached New Zealand, during the last week of June, Marian felt much better, pronouncing the concert in Wellington on the twenty-fifth "the best concert on the tour." But the New Zealand critics felt differently. Indeed, they were so harsh in their criticism as to cause one interviewer in New Zealand to ask Marian "whether she felt any resentment at having received such criticisms after so distinguished a career?" "No, I don't at all," she answered. "I think anyone who wished to write is there because someone feels he is in a position to write. And the person writes very often his personal feelings about it. As long as he is sincere about his personal feelings, he's at liberty to write it for the paper. You can't go around and say, 'Don't write that,' or 'I don't like that,' or 'I don't like it,' or whatever."

Marian arrived home in mid-July, having looked forward for months to spending the rest of the summer with King. Less than a month later, the calm of Marianna was shattered by the news that Jimmy, who had spent most of the year in the Far East as an American specialist for the State Department, had contracted polio in Thailand, only a few weeks before his scheduled return to the States. For the moment, all Jimmy wanted to do was to get home. "Somebody please get me home," he telegraphed his mother at the end of August. Marian contacted Edward R. Murrow, then head of the USIA, asking him to do what he could to get Jimmy back to the States as quickly as possible.

In Bangkok on September 4, Jimmy was loaded by stretcher on to a US military cargo plane headed for Clark Air Force Base in the Philippines. Flying through thunder and rainstorms while lying on a stretcher, for twelve hours among seriously wounded medical evacuees from Viet Nam, Jimmy found the journey to be a nightmare. In the States, he was admitted to Magee Rehabilitation Hospital, a nationally ranked specialty hospital in Philadelphia. Jimmy was paralyzed from the waist down, requiring braces and crutches to walk.

"Now that I know what I want to do," he told Leonard Bernstein, "I can't do it." Assuring Jimmy that he would surmount his physical limitations if conducting was what he really wanted, Bernstein advised him to enter the Mitropoulos conducting competition scheduled to take place in two years. Bernstein's advice and the belief and encouragement he showed the younger musician proved to be the foundation of Jimmy's career. On December 12, 1964, six winners of the conducting competition were selected from a field of thirty-six contestants from eighteen countries. They each conducted the contest's Orchestra of America before a panel of judges headed by Mr. Bernstein. The competition had started on November 30, 1964. Jimmy was one of two Americans among the six winners; finishing in the top three overall, he qualified for one of the three assistant conductor positions the following season with the New York Philharmonic Orchestra.

The year that started poorly ended the same way. In November, Marian took part in a Lincoln Center tribute for her dear departed friend Mrs. Roosevelt, who had recently died, sponsored by the Eleanor Roosevelt Memorial Foundation.

- **1963** – Prior to the historic March on Washington for Jobs and Freedom on August 28, Marian was invited by Roy Wilkins, Executive Director of the NAACP to sing the national anthem. Unfortunately, due to the larger than expected crowd and traffic jams throughout the Washington area, she was not able to arrive at the Lincoln Memorial platform on time to sing. Roy Wilkins, who noticed Camilla Williams standing at the front of the huge crowd, motioned her to come up to the platform to sing instead. Later during the event, however, Marian did sing "He's Got the Whole World in His Hands."

  There were many other pop singing artists whose performances were more appreciated by the younger generation crowd. At the march, The Rev. Dr. Martin Luther King Jr. delivered his inspirational "I Have a Dream" speech, which envisioned a world where people were judged not by the color of their skin but by the content of their character. While concluding his speech, Dr. King recited the exact same words that he had heard as a ten-year old boy from Marian's opening song in 1939 on those same steps (*"My Country, 'tis of thee, sweet land of liberty …,"* etc.).

  Marian's overall disappointment with the way things turned out in Washington came at a difficult time, as she was struggling with the realization that she could not postpone her retirement much longer. By the fall she was ready to meet with Hurok to discuss concrete plans for a final tour. For his part, Hurok did not want Marian's career to simply dwindle to a close in a way that would not draw the kind of publicity and sense of celebration he believed appropriate.

Discussions that fall centered around the idea of a world tour and the strategies necessary for securing the best dates and the largest fees. Marian was prepared to announce her retirement during those months, but Hurok wanted to hold out for the right opportunity that would focus media attention on the announcement. In July, Marian had been chosen as one of thirty-one recipients for the Presidential Medal of Freedom, an honor that might provide the kind of opportunity Hurok was looking for.

1963 – On December 6, just two weeks after the death of President Kennedy, Marian was awarded the Presidential Medal of Freedom—America's highest civilian honor—by President Johnson, as Kennedy had originally planned to do. Overall, the medal is awarded for "especially meritorious contributions to the security or national interest of the United States, world peace, cultural or other significant public or private endeavors." Marian's citation read "Artist and citizen, she has ennobled her race and her country, while her voice has enthralled the world." In the *New York Times* the following day, the sole photograph of the entire ceremony captured a radiantly smiling Marian Anderson together with President Johnson.

For Hurok, timing was everything. Hastened into action by the White House ceremony and the prominence awarded Marian in the *Times*, Hurok planned a press conference for December 12 to announce her retirement. They faced a bank of reporters at the St. Regis Hotel in New York to announce her retirement from the concert stage after a world tour beginning the following fall in 1964.

For both Marian and Hurok, the press conference was an emotional experience anchored in a relationship that stretched back nearly thirty years. In introducing Marian, Hurok recalled some of the incidents when hotels and restaurants refused her service because of her color. There were the inevitable questions from the press about Marian's feelings toward the DAR.

"I forgave the DAR many years ago. You lose a lot of time hating people," she sensibly told the reporters. Although plans for the extensive world tour were still being developed, Hurok announced Marian's farewell tour in the States scheduled to commence on Easter Sunday, April 8, 1965, at Carnegie Hall. Asked about her plans for retirement, Marian said they included becoming more active in the civil rights struggle. "The position of the Negro artist was good today," she told reporters, "study opportunities were better, and the concert field was open."

To distract from her pending retirement, the support she could count on from her family and friends who gathered each year in Danbury for Christmas and New Year's was replaced now by concern over the increasing seriousness of Mrs. Anderson's health. Ethel and Alyse had decided to remain on Martin Street this holiday season, as Mrs. Anderson was far too frail to travel to Danbury.

- **1964** – Shortly after the new year began, on January 10, Anna Anderson died of heart failure at the age of eighty-nine. She was Marian's closest friend and confident, so this was a heavy blow. By eleven o'clock on the thirteenth, during a blizzard, a large crowd of family and friends made their way to Tindley Temple United Methodist Church at 750 South Broad Street to pay their last respects to Anna Anderson. Through her dedication and dignity, Anna had endeared herself to many generations of Tindley Temple's congregation.

In the early afternoon, in the driving snow and sleet, the funeral procession made their way to the Anderson family plot, just outside Philadelphia, at Eden Cemetery in Collingdale, Delaware County, Pennsylvania, where Anna Anderson was laid to rest to await the eventual arrival of her three daughters to also be "promoted to glory."

In the weeks and months following her mother's death, Marian coped, as always, by throwing herself into her work. In February, she began work on an album of popular songs as part of a project in collaboration with composer Robert Russell Bennett. The Bennett arrangements were one of a series of four long-playing records Marian had agreed to record for RCA during the months leading up to her farewell tour.

Hurok, as always, was counting on the publication of new recordings to attract attention and provide publicity. Marian wanted to leave a final legacy of recordings that would reflect a wide-ranging repertoire and variety of styles. In addition to the Bennett arrangements, Marian had committed herself to an album of Schubert lieder and another of Brahms lieder, as well as a new recording of spirituals.

1964 – October 24 began her sold-out farewell concert tour at Constitution Hall. To heighten the significance, it had been decided—here again one can imagine Hurok's influence—that the opening concert would be recorded and issued by RCA as soon as possible. At the advice of counsel, the DAR would only allow the recording if RCA agreed to make no mention of past recitals and experiences. Ten days before the concert the DAR had not relented, and RCA was not willing to concede. Marian felt a refusal might create an unfortunate situation and unnecessary publicity that would serve no useful purpose, so she asked RCA to comply. From Washington the six-month tour went from coast to coast and fifty cities across the nation.

- **1965** – On Easter Sunday, April 18, Marian concluded her farewell concert tour at Carnegie Hall, where she had given over fifty concerts since her return to America thirty years before. She was greeted by a huge, cheering sold-out house overflowing onto the stage. There were many celebrities in the audience as well as two hundred friends and family members seated in the specially reserved boxes Marian had arranged for them. At the end of the concert, after her last encore with the audience still refusing to leave, Marian seemed pensive. Hurok urged her to sing again, to which she replied merely, "No. It's finished."

The unrestrained enthusiasm of the sell-out audiences throughout the United States during Marian's farewell tour was the kind of incentive that always stimulated Hurok's imagination. "She doesn't have to sing," he told reporters after Marian's farewell concert at Carnegie Hall. "She can do some readings of Lincoln and Jefferson and then maybe sing a few spirituals. It'll go like a house on fire." Marian thought the idea appealing enough to try it out in the summer of 1965.

Whatever confluence of emotions Marian felt at the end of the tour, it was her sister Alyse who was most on her mind, and in the succeeding weeks the gradual worsening of Alyse's health absorbed her attention. For years, Alyse had suffered from anemia and more recently had waged a quiet courageous battle with leukemia. The doctor suggested she be hospitalized and a few days later, Marian took her to the hospital. On the ninth, a heart specialist was brought in, and a blood transfusion was ordered.

On May 21, Alyse died of heart failure. The funeral mass was held three days later at St. Charles, the neighborhood Roman Catholic church, a large prominent church near Rittenhouse Square, where Alyse had worshipped. After her hospitalization at Eagleville in 1953 she had found a haven in the Roman Catholic Church and had converted to Catholicism. Among the letters of condolence the family received was one from James H. J. Tate, the mayor of Philadelphia, who learned of Alyse's illness through the clergy at St. Patrick's R.C. Church.

Although Marian had formerly announced her "retirement," the reality was that she had committed herself to several additional concerts. At the end of June, she sang for the first time with her nephew, James DePriest, who had been asked to conduct the Philadelphia Orchestra at the Robin Hood Dell, Philadelphia's only outdoor amphitheater at the time. After winning the Mitropoulos competition the previous December, DePriest had been chosen by Leonard Bernstein, the conductor of the New York Philharmonic, to be one of his assistants.

Coming so soon after Alyse's death, the concert was a great strain on Marian, but she never considered withdrawing. Thinking that the Dell concert would be the only opportunity to perform with his Aunt Marian, DePriest wanted her to sing, as he later recalled, "absolutely everything that he admired about Aunt Marian's art." More than generous in accommodating her nephew's unrestrained enthusiasm, Marian and DePriest performed the Brahms *Four Serious Songs*, arias from *Un ballo in maschera* and *Samson et Dalila*, Schubert's "Ave Maria," and a group of spirituals Jimmy himself arranged for the orchestra. Max de Schauensee, the critic from the *Philadelphia Evening Bulletin*, who had been attending concerts in the Dell for twenty-five years, wrote the next day that he had never seen such a large crowd "struggling into the auditorium."

At a Lewisohn Stadium concert with Arthur Fiedler and the Metropolitan Opera Orchestra on the eve of Independence Day, as part of a program featuring the music of American composers, Marian narrated Aaron Copland's *Lincoln Portrait* for the first time and sang a group of spirituals Hall Johnson had arranged for her for the recording of *Jus' Keep On Singin'*.

A Lincoln Portrait, in which Marian appeared as narrator for more than a decade, held tremendous appeal for her. Although for the younger, more outspoken, more militant generation of the 1960s, Lincoln's image had lost a great deal of its significance, Marian, like most blacks of her generation, felt deeply in the force of his words and his deeds, and she was able to communicate this feeling to her audiences. She spoke Lincoln's words with directness and fervor, without any trace of exaggeration differentiating Lincoln's voice from that of the narrator. In the famous concluding lines, "that government of the people, by the people, for the people shall not perish from the earth," Marian achieved a level of intensity audiences found extraordinarily moving.

Marian's performances of *A Lincoln Portrait* generated considerable excitement, not only because of her interpretive abilities but also because of the historic association stemming from the events surrounding the 1939 Lincoln Memorial concert, events that many who came to hear her no doubt remembered.

The narrating of Copland's work was a fortunate choice for Marian at this time of her life. She was able to receive artistic satisfaction from a relatively brief work, one that did not overly depend on her singing voice and that reduced her worldwide travel away from home, so she could spend more time with King. Her performances also brought in regular income since maintaining Marianna was costly, more so than ever, and she was able to maintain her family responsibilities and philanthropic interests.

Since serving as a delegate to the United Nations, Marian was interested in doing what she could to help the people in Africa. She was, therefore, only too happy to participate in a fundraising event in support of the First World African Festival of the Arts, planned for April 1966, in Dakar.

The idea of the festival, conceived by Leopold Senghor, the president of Senegal, was to bring together leading black figures from around the world, scholars as well as artists, to showcase the great achievements, both traditional and modern, of the African people. Marian was invited to sing a program of spirituals in the Sainte-Chapelle in Paris.

Before leaving for Paris, Marian had received an invitation from the US Navy and Newport News Shipbuilding and Dry Dock Company, to be the sponsor for the Navy's newest nuclear-powered ballistic-missile submarine, the USS *George Washington Carver* (SSBN 656). She christened the ship at Newport News, Virginia, on August 14, 1965.

In September 1965, Marian and John Motley, whom she wanted as her accompanist for the concert, flew to Paris for several days. They rehearsed the program on the twenty-seventh. The concert the next evening attracted a glamorous audience of French celebrities and African diplomats—President Senghor was present—all willing to pay $100 to attend the recital and the showing of the film *Carmen James*. For the half-hour program, Marian and Motley performed sixteen spirituals, ending with "He's Got the Whole World in His Hands."

- **1966** – On July 9 and 10, in a concert at Grand Park, Illinois, with the Chicago Symphony Orchestra conducted by DePriest, Marian sang for the last time in public. She narrated Aaron Copland's *Preamble for a Solemn Occasion* and, at the end of the program, offered a group of spirituals. For half a century, since Marian's performance that afternoon in 1915 when she sang with the other students of Mary Saunders Patterson, music had been her deepest passion and sacred responsibility. It was left to her nephew, Jimmy, now to embody those ideals.

In December 1966, President Johnson appointed Marian as one of eight new members to the National Council of the Arts. In the end, retirement for Marian was a gradual process. While far from becoming the housewife she had imagined, she spent more time together with King going to horse shows, or to the theatre, and to others' performances. Tony Bennett was a particular favorite of hers.

Professionally, during the 1960s and most of the 1970s, Marian remained a Hurok narration artist and was assigned to the lecture bureau that Hurok managed as part of his agency. As lecturer, she spoke at colleges and music conservatories and at various commemorative occasions, her speeches were prepared mostly by writers attached to Hurok's lecture bureau.

Particularly memorable were those occasions on which she performed with Copland himself and with her nephew, Jimmy. Marian's desire to stay in the public eye, as well as to bring in regular income motivated her to continue working, but she began to feel the strain of performing and lecturing.

During her concert tours, Hurok had always provided her with a traveling manager, but those days were over. Now in her seventies, Marian would often have to travel to an engagement on her own, carrying her own luggage and fighting the crowds at Grand Central Station in New York. Her health remained remarkably robust, but she began to suffer from high blood pressure, sometimes arriving back at Marianna more than usually strained.

- **1969** – On a chilly winter day, as Marian was leaving Wanamaker's Department Store in downtown Philadelphia, she encountered several young girls on the street outside the store trying to sell their Girl Scout cookies to the pedestrians and motorists driving by. As a former Camp Fire Girl herself, Marian decided she would help them sell cookies. It was quite a picture: the girls in their uniforms and overcoats and Marian in a full-length mink coat hawking cookies! Marian learned during their conversation that while the boys had a nice warm clubhouse, the girls had none. Soon thereafter, Marian privately funded construction of a Girl Scouts of America Club House, which no doubt was designed by King.[4] At the time, the young girls probably had no idea who the nice lady was helping them sell cookies, but a motorist passing by noticed it was Marian Anderson selling cookies with the Girl Scouts. That motorist, Jules Schick, an off-duty photographer for the *Philadelphia Evening Bulletin*, took a photograph and privately mailed it to Marian. Until now, that photograph has never been published.

- **1973** – Marian was now at an age when many of her friends were dying off. Most notably, Billy King, her first accompanist and longtime, somewhat estranged friend, had his first stroke in 1973; he died in early 1975.

- **1974** – Sol Hurok wound up suddenly dropping dead on a street in downtown Manhattan at the age of eighty-five on March 5, 1974. His funeral took place in Carnegie Hall, where, on March 9, more than 2,600 people bid farewell to the impresario extraordinaire. Isaac Stern, long associated with Hurok, played a Bach Partita; then Jan Peerce, also a longtime friend and associate, after asking the audience to rise, sang a Jewish hymn made up of Psalms.

Marian delivered the eulogy. "He launched hundreds of careers," Marian said; "he magnified thousands of others, and in the process, he brought joy and a larger life to millions. He made not ripples, but waves, even beyond his own shores, and what is one to say of the man who guided one's own life for nigh on to forty years? He was more than the supreme impresario. He was teacher, counsel, friend and even more than that, he was the 'we' in all of us."

1974 – By now, the summertime Philadelphia concerts had outgrown the Robin Hood Dell East venue. Marian anonymously contributed $2.5 million to help build a new additional venue for her fellow Philadelphians in 1976: The Robin Hood Dell West, renamed in 1979 as The Mann Music Center. (Today in 2020 dollars, this is equivalent to $15.2 million.)[3,4]

•   **1975** – Children's Hospital of Philadelphia (CHOP) is a world-renowned charitable, nonprofit hospital, making tomorrow's breakthroughs possible for children today from around the world. No doubt, Marian's love for children and generous heart led her to anonymously contribute several million dollars toward the construction of the new modern expanded hospital. (In 2020 dollars, she reportedly gave over $15 million.)[3,4]

~ Marian Anderson always gave generously and quietly – never for naming rights – Always out of gratitude for those who helped in the early days of her career, and to glorify her Creator for the gift of her God-given voice ~

1975 – Now they were in their declining years, and shortly after New Year's Day, following a mild stroke at home, King was hospitalized. While in the hospital he suffered a more serious stroke which left him with paralysis on his right side, mostly in his leg, and with a moaning kind of speech. King's condition improved gradually and, in a few weeks, he was transferred to the Rusk Institute of Rehabilitation in Manhattan. After several weeks of therapy, his speech improved dramatically. After a few weeks back home, he regained some mobility and, with difficulty, was able to walk with assistance.

Marian often found the strain of caring for King at home arduous. For the first few years she employed part-time nurse's aides, and she eventually hired a regular part-time housekeeper, Ruth Ingaren, but in the evenings, Marian took care of King herself. He was a large man, and it was no small task for Marian to help him in and out of bed and around the house. After a while, King was able to walk more easily, but his unsteadiness sometimes caused him to fall, and Marian would have to struggle to lift him up and get him into bed.

King's illness convinced Marian that only by selling Marianna could she acquire sufficient capital to pay for the expense of his full-time home care for the years ahead. The home and remaining forty-six-acre farm were sold to a developer, who agreed to a plan allowing Marian and King to live there as rent-paying tenants for as long as they liked.

- **1976** – For a few years after King's strokes, Marian continued to make appearances as both a narrator and speaker, but the physical effort of travel began to take a greater and greater toll on her health. After a performance in Dallas with the Dance Theatre of Harlem, Marian arrived home physically exhausted, exhibiting a rise in blood pressure and slurred speech. With medication to bring down her blood pressure, she recovered quickly from what the doctor treating her assumed was hypertension and a vascular spasm. A few months later, after a performance of *A Lincoln Portrait*, there was a similar incident, this time a little worse.

- **1977** – Around the time of the previous year's Dallas episode, plans for a Carnegie Hall gala celebration of Marian's seventy-fifth birthday had just gotten underway. Out of concern expressed by the hall's management about whether Marian could attend, her doctor assured them that in view of how well she was responding to medication, he saw no reason why plans for the concert could not go ahead.

On her birthday, February 27, with an audience that was, in the words of the *New York Times* story the next day, "pure Marian Anderson—some luminaries, some family members, children, adults, black and white," Marian, a little frail and not quite herself, celebrated what was publicly thought to be her seventy-fifth birthday but what was, in reality, her eightieth, since past publicists had mistakenly listed her date of birth as 1902 instead of 1897.

The Carnegie Hall concert, the proceeds of which were to go, at Marian's request, to 'Young Audiences,' had been planned as an occasion for bringing together performers with a strong personal connection to Marian Anderson—the singers Leontyne Price and Shirley Verrett, as well as members of the Dance Theatre of Harlem, an organization for which Marian felt strong affection because of the importance it placed on providing young students with high quality education, the best training for the lowest possible tuition.

In the end, the concert became the setting for an extended series of tributes celebrating far more than Marian's status as an artist. Henry Labouisse, executive director of UNICEF, recalling Marian's service as a United Nations delegate, presented her with the United Nations Peace Prize. New York's Mayor Beame presented her with the Handel Medallion for her cultural contributions "to the city, the country and the world." The First Lady of the United States, Rosalynn Carter, with whom Marian and some of her family were sharing a box, presented her with President Carter's birthday wishes and informed her—and the vast audience in the hall—of the congressional resolution that had been passed the previous Friday authorizing the Treasury Department to strike a gold medal in Marian's honor for her "untiring and unselfish devotion to the promotion of the arts in this country during a distinguished and impressive career of more than half a century."

• **1978** – The actual presentation by President Carter of the Congressional Gold Medal took place much later, in August, in a small ceremony at the White House. To coincide with that presentation, and as part of the worldwide commemoration of the 150th anniversary of Schubert's death, RCA Records released a long-playing album of Schubert and Brahms lieder recorded by Marian in 1966 only months before her seventieth birthday. The album seems to have produced little critical comment one way or another, yet her voice exhibited a surprising freshness and bloom in comparison with the Constitution Hall farewell recital the previous year. Marian produced a series of interpretations in which each Schubert and Brahms song was inhabited with the wisdom and truthfulness of a lifetime's experience of lieder singing.

Still, this was a curious release made by RCA. Since the issuing of a series of recordings around the time of Marian's farewell tour, in 1964–65, which had included the reappearance of some of her important lieder recordings of the 1930s and 1940s, there had not been a single reissue by RCA of any of Marian Anderson's earlier records. There were, and undoubtedly still are, any number of recordings in RCA's vaults—Schubert and Brahms lieder, the series of Sibelius songs, Schumann's *Frauenliebe und -leben*—which, at that point, had been denied to the public for more than thirty years and would have done more to honor her unique qualities as a singer. (To date, the public has been denied these recordings for close to eighty-five years! One wonders why RCA Records and now its successor, Sony Music Entertainment, has chosen this course of inaction.)

Indeed, the legend of Marian Anderson, already written into the social consciousness of the country, was perhaps beginning to obscure the memory of Marian Anderson the artist, the record of her singing now kept alive more by individual memory and official tribute than by any consistent effort by those controlling her recordings to keep her most important and representative recordings before the public. Sony Music Entertainment, the successor to RCA Records, has yet to address this oversight.

The demands on Marian's time hardly abated during her eighties, whether to accept awards or honorary degrees, to talk to young people in colleges or conservatories, or to devote time to arts organizations. Bouts of unsteadiness, or episodes of acute hypertension that brought on temporary vascular spasms affecting her speech, made her wary of traveling. Otherwise, it was not in her nature to say no.

1978 – The Kennedy Center Honors is an annual honor given to those in the performing arts for their lifetime of contributions to American culture. The honors have been presented annually since 1978, culminating each December in a star-studded gala celebrating the honorees in the Kennedy Center Opera House in Washington, DC. Marian Anderson was among the pioneering artists to receive this honor during its inaugural awards ceremony.

• **1979** – In August, at the age of eighty-two, Marian made her last onstage appearance at Philadelphia's Mann Music Center during a concert performed by Luciano Pavarotti. That evening, according to an eyewitness in the audience, Marian received an award from the University of Pennsylvania. She had donated her lifelong collection of personal papers, records, memorabilia, and photographs to Penn's library two years earlier. Today, this professionally curated and catalogued collection of the Marian Anderson Papers has been digitized and is available for viewing online at https://penntoday.upenn.edu/news/newly-digitized-marian-anderson-collection-now-accessible-online. For direct access to the Marian Anderson Collection: https://mariananderson.exhibits.library.upenn.edu/

- **1982** – A month before her eighty-fifth birthday, Marian attended a gala concert in her honor at Carnegie Hall, where she heard arias and duets by Grace Bumbry and Shirley Verrett and greetings from Mayor Koch and from President Reagan, read by Isaac Stern.

- **1984** – In July, at a City Hall ceremony in New York, Marian accepted the first Eleanor Roosevelt Human Rights Award. Mayor Koch had to help her up from her wheelchair, but once on her feet, Marian stood on her own at the podium and told those present, "I have thanked my good Lord for her many times. I'm only sorry the youngsters of today shall not have seen her in the flesh." At the end of the ceremony, when the roomful of guests sang "He's Got the Whole World in His Hands," Marian wept.

  After the onset of King's illness, Marian had written to King's son, James, who had not visited his father for some time, urging him to come to the farm. Despite James's reconciliation with his father some years earlier, he still felt enough bitterness to keep him away for long periods. Finally, James's own son urged him to patch things up again. James never forgot how, in his first visit to the farm in years, "King cried like a baby."

  Marian had pastimes that kept her occupied on her own. She liked to work on sewing projects or spend time in her darkroom developing pictures. Most important, however, for King as well as Marian, now that they were more sedentary than either had been used to, were those occasions where there was company, whether visits arranged carefully in advance or impromptu social calls.

  Marian took special pleasure in the visits of children. Whenever anyone brought a child to see her, the child would immediately gain center stage. Jannette De Fazio, who came to work for Marian as a part-time secretary in 1982, later recalled that Marian "could care less if she got any work done on Thursdays" when she brought her granddaughter Nicole with her to work; Marian "wanted to watch the baby and to hold her."

Marian was also visited by younger as well as more established black singers— "my girls," as she always called them—and these visitors joined the same inner circle as neighbors' children or grandchildren. Jessye Norman and Kathleen Battle came to Marianna to meet Marian and to tell her of their success in the world of opera. John Motley was a frequent visitor and the only one of Marian's friends who could get her to sing, as he played the piano for her. Marian stayed in touch with Franz Rupp, now in his eighties as well, but she did not see him very often since Franz's first wife, Steffi, died in 1976, and he was now happily remarried, this time to a much younger woman, Sylvia Stone, who, no less than Steffi, indulged his every wish.

Gradually, King's health worsened. He could no longer walk on his own, even with help; round-the-clock nurse attendants in eight-hour shifts were required. King's doctor as well as family and friends tried to convince Marian that it would be far easier on everyone if King were in a nursing home. After a while she gave in, and King did go to a nursing home, but after a few weeks Marian could not stand how miserable he felt away from home. He longed to be back at Marianna where he could sit in the dining room or library and look out at the trees and the flowers. After a few weeks, Marian brought him home. Whenever the subject of a nursing home came up again, Marian refused to consider it. "I want to be able to put my head on the pillow at night and sleep peacefully," she said.

- **1986** – President Reagan awarded Marian the National Medal of the Arts—the highest honor given to artists and arts patrons by the United States government—as "special recognition by reason of their outstanding contributions to the excellence, growth, support and availability of the arts in the United States."

1986 – In the middle of March, King contracted pneumonia and was taken to Danbury Hospital. After a week or so he appeared to be out of danger and was expected to come home, but in the early morning of March 26, at the age of eighty-five, he died suddenly of cardiopulmonary arrest. King and Marian had been married for forty-three years. Marian arranged a small memorial service for him at the New Hope Baptist Church in Danbury, which King had designed and where he had been a member for many years. Among those who gathered in the chapel were King's son James, his sister Pauline, and Robert O'Neill, a nephew.

For a while after King's death, Marian thought of moving back to Philadelphia to live with Ethel on Martin Street. The idea had come up several times through the years. But Marian, like King, really wanted to be able to see the trees and the flowers blossom around Marianna in the spring and to enjoy the summers in the country. Marianna had been Marian's home for forty-six years, and she was not able to think seriously of pulling up roots now that she was approaching ninety.

Ethel was now more than ever a comfort to Marian. They had established a bond of communication over the years that continued to serve them well. Every evening Marian called Martin Street, as she had done since she began touring half a century before. For the holidays—Easter, Thanksgiving, and Christmas—Ethel came to Marianna, staying at Christmas until after the new year, and during the summers Ethel spent several weeks at Marianna. Although it was becoming more difficult for Marian to travel, she rarely complained about being lonely. The round-the-clock nurses that cared for her, especially those she grew particularly fond of, were as much companions as active caregivers.

Marian also had frequent visitors. One was June Goodman, an old Danbury friend. They had known each other for more than forty years but had become much closer since June had enlisted Marian's aid in laying the groundwork and raising money for the Charles Ives Performing Arts Center. Another frequent visitor was Sandra Grymes, a cousin of Marian's, to whom she always referred lovingly as her niece. Sandra came in from New

York whenever she could to see Marian and tell her about the latest happenings on the music scene.

June and Sandra shared Jimmy's missionary zeal about the importance of keeping alive the record of Marian's greatness as a singer, which all three felt should remain at the center of Marian's legacy. Marian was never a willing ally when plans to focus publicly on her life and achievements came up. Having lived her life and contributed what she could, she never pondered over her legacy. "Aunt Marian had no expectation," Jimmy later recalled, "that people would or should remember what she accomplished, and she was always surprised when it happened."

Nevertheless, others pressed on. June wanted Marian to be honored by Danbury in the form of an annual award established in her name that would be given to promising young American singers. In a way, June thought, this would revive the award Marian herself had established in Philadelphia in the 1940s, rendering permanent tribute to Marian's work in promoting the careers of young singers. June helped convince the Charles Ives Center to establish a Marian Anderson Celebration Committee to raise money to finance the endowment for the award.

With June as the chairwoman and Isaac Stern as honorary chairman, the committee began a two-year fund-raising campaign with a goal of $500,000. As part of the fundraising, the Ives Center suggested a gala concert in Marian's honor—to which she was loath to agree, simply thinking no one would come. But on August 13, 1989, despite the threat of thunderstorms, 2,500 people gathered at the Ives Center to hear Jessye Norman, Isaac Stern, and Julius Rudel and the Ives Symphony Orchestra. "I know enough not to speak after Isaac Stern," Marian told the audience. "So, I shall say to you from the bottom of my heart, I thank you; I love you." A year later, Sylvia McNair became the first recipient of the Charles Ives Performing Arts Center's Marian Anderson Award.

- **1989** – The Philadelphia Music Alliance inducts their grand hometown lady, Marian Anderson, into their "Walk of Fame."

1989 – Early in the year, WETA, the public radio and television station in Washington, DC, as part of its cultural affairs programming, approached Jimmy with the idea of developing a television documentary about Marian Anderson's life. Marian objected to the idea, but in the end, Jimmy talked her into it.

In order to coax her into becoming more at ease with the idea, and to enlist her help in the difficult project of establishing the factual background for the documentary, Jimmy took advantage of one of Ethel's visits to Marianna to encourage his mother and Marian to reminisce about their early years in South Philadelphia and the beginnings of Marian's career. One morning during breakfast, Jimmy set up a small tape recorder in the dining room and urged the two to start from the beginning, prompting them with questions and encouraging them to be accurate about when things happened. Ethel enjoyed the experience, providing details about growing up, recalling favorite stories, and scolding Jimmy for being impatient with the leisurely pace she adopted. Marian rarely entered into the spirit of the casual fun around the table, weighing what she said more seriously and deliberately than Ethel.

During the summer when the WETA film crew came up to Marianna to begin filming Marian's portion of the documentary, it was Jimmy who asked the questions and encouraged her to talk, and that helped considerably to relax her.

- **1990** – In many ways, Ethel, with her prodigious memory of events that had taken place more than half a century before, proved to be the family historian for the project. Sadly, she did not live to see the completed documentary. She came up from Philadelphia around Christmastime, as she did each year. Having planned to stay for a week or two into the new year, she complained about not feeling well and decided to return home early. A few weeks later, she suffered a brain aneurysm and was taken to Jefferson Hospital. Although she had just turned eighty-eight on January 14, she had been in surprisingly good health, and the doctors were pleased with her rapid progress. Yet on February 1, with hardly any warning, Ethel died of complications brought on by the aneurysm. Marian rarely revealed a great deal about how she felt, but there was no mistaking how shattered she was by Ethel's death. She grieved deeply.

Gradually in the weeks and months following, Marian pulled herself together and went on. Having agreed to participate in the WETA documentary, she made no objection to a second series of interviews in June.

- **1991** – The Recording Academy honored Marian with their Grammy Lifetime Achievement Award. This is a special Grammy Award reserved for "performers who, during their lifetimes, have made creative contributions of outstanding artistic significance to the field of recording."

1991 – In May, two months after celebrating her ninety-fourth birthday, she traveled to the Kennedy Center for a private showing of the film *Marian Anderson*, narrated by Avery Brooks.

Early in the day, before the film showing that evening, Marian, accompanied by Jimmy and Sharon Percy Rockefeller, the president of WETA, went to the White House for tea with Mrs. Bush and a photo session with President Bush.

A few nights later, the film was shown on public television. Its reception was mixed. One critic found the accounts of Marian by friends and associates—they included Franz Rupp, Patrick Hayes, members of Union Baptist Church, and opera singers Jessye Norman and Mattiwilda Dobbs—"wearily worshipful," yet at the same time, like most viewers, was struck by the immense dignity of her every appearance throughout the film.

The finished version of Marian's beautiful life story, expertly cowritten by Juan Williams (now a FOX TV host), can be seen here: https://www.youtube.com/watch?v=nH4cffnJUow

Later that summer, at a routine examination at Danbury Hospital, doctors discovered the early signs of bowel cancer. Marian found the doctors there too aggressive and made it clear that she did not want surgery or the intervention of machines. She wished only to remain at home and to be made as comfortable as possible.

One of Marian's friends suggested that she be seen by Dr. Micheline Williams, a Danbury physician. Although too busy to make house calls, Dr. Williams agreed to see Marian at Marianna. "I don't want to be treated for anything they find," she told Dr. Williams, who found Marian delightful and fascinating to listen to, although obviously lonely. Before long, the doctor noticed how much Marian was anticipating her visits, and often they were as much social calls as examinations.

Marian would have been content to live out the remainder of her life at Marianna, but Jimmy and his wife, Ginette, wanted Marian to be with them in Portland, Oregon. They were worried about her well-being and wanted to look after her themselves. For the short time left for Marian, Jimmy wanted her to be with family. He talked the idea over with Dr. Williams, and both agreed it was a good idea. Marian gradually came to accept the move as God's will, agreeing, with mixed emotions, to move to Portland.

- **1992** – During the months of packing, Marian gradually became more comfortable with the idea. June, Sandra, and Jeanette De Fazio took charge of most of the work, helping Marian sort through a lifetime of accumulations. The fact that Wilhelmina Fortnos, one of Marian's nurse attendants whom she especially liked, would be able to remain indefinitely with Marian in Portland added immeasurably to her sense of comfort. Mush,

Marian's cat, would also be making the trip with her, providing another comforting link between Marianna and Portland.

On July 6, 1992, a few days before Marian was scheduled to fly to Portland, she suffered another vascular spasm. She refused to go to the hospital and by the next day had recovered well. On the morning of July 9, Jimmy and Ginette, who had flown to Connecticut to accompany Marian on the trip, flew with her to Portland, along with Wilhelmina. Mush went along in a cat carrier.

Surprising to all, Marian adjusted quickly and well to her new surroundings. Friends who traveled to Portland to visit her invariably found her content and looking healthier than during her last months at Marianna. Ginette doted on her even more than Jimmy. June Goodman, having carefully packed in dry ice Marian's favorite chocolate raspberry ice cream, made the trip in the fall, and at Thanksgiving, Eleanor Peters, one of Marian's oldest friends, came up from Los Angeles to be with her.

• **1993** – On February 27, Marian celebrated her ninety-sixth birthday. She had been feeling more tired than usual and not eating as well as she had been but talked on the phone throughout the day to friends offering birthday wishes. During the next month, her health declined considerably. In March she suffered an epileptic seizure. Her doctor prescribed a seizure drug and tried to make her as comfortable as possible. Ginette, who was with Jimmy in Sweden, where he was giving concerts, came home immediately, as soon as they got word of Marian's illness.

Marian rallied a bit over the next few weeks, but near the end of March another seizure occurred, and, by then having lost her speech, she began to slip in and out of a coma. Jimmy canceled his remaining concerts and arrived home around the first of April. During the weeks before Jimmy's return Ginette had slept in Marian's room so she would not be alone. Once home, Jimmy took up the vigil. On Wednesday evening, April 7, Jimmy had a concert in Salem with the Oregon Symphony Orchestra.

Somehow, when he got home, he had a premonition that his Aunt Marian would not make it through the night. He had been studying the score of Mahler's Tenth Symphony at the time. Perhaps it was his preoccupation with Mahler's last work, which the composer left unfinished, that heightened his awareness. He spent the rest of the night in Marian's room, sitting at the desk. Around 4:30 on the morning of April 8, Marian Anderson died. She was finally "Promoted to Glory," to be with the rest of her family, forever in heaven!

1993 – The passing of Marian Anderson was covered that day on national television. See it here: https://www.youtube.com/watch?v=CeJaLdczses

1993 – On a warm and bright Sunday morning in June, more than two hundred people made their way to the Union Baptist Church at Nineteenth and Fitzwater Streets in South Philadelphia, across from the Anderson home on Martin Street, near the Rittenhouse Square area. They had gathered there to pay their respects and attend a memorial service for their beloved Marian Anderson. Inside the church, there was a relaxed and genial atmosphere as family members who had not seen each other for a long time greeted each other, old friends embraced, and older members of the congregation shared with each other and their children their feeling of pride of how much Union Baptist had done to nurture the extraordinary talent of "our Marian."

The Reverend Gregory L. Wallace, the church's pastor, told all those present: "Back in the first decade of this century, the members in this church saw in Marian Anderson the gifts of God. They saw in her what others had seen in Beethoven and Shakespeare, and perhaps even in Michelangelo. We have all been blessed by her music of the soul, music that transcends time. The members of this church heard in that voice the grace and benediction that only God can give."

Sandra Grymes, Marian's niece, spoke at the service about how Marian and her sisters were "trained to cast a stoic face upon gratuitous insults." She also spoke about Marian's inner faith "that made her stronger than all of us" and about how Marian's "trips into the world and her returns to us enlarged our vision of our individual possibilities."

The last to share his memories on Marian was Jimmy. He was mindful of Marian's admonition about the way she wanted to be remembered. She had said to him, "No fuss." So now Jimmy spoke without fuss, telling stories of what it was like growing up on Martin Street in a family defined by love and faith and the strength of determined women, Aunt Marian among them. Jimmy told the gathering about the importance of Union Baptist Church in his family's life. "They had wonderful times in this church," he said, "and this is essentially why we are here today. This church is central to our lives, central to our faith, central to everything we did." Finally, Jimmy spoke of Marian's voice. "No one could pay tribute to Marian Anderson better than my Aunt Marian herself," he said, "with that extraordinary voice that seems to come from the center of each of us."

As he walked away from the podium, Marian's voice rose up, filling Union Baptist Church with the words of the spirituals she loved—"Deep River," "Crucifixion," and finally, "He's Got the Whole World in His Hands." For those gathered there, she accomplished what she had always accomplished. With her voice, she lifted their spirits.

1993 – Marian was laid to rest in her family's plot at Historic Eden Cemetery, close to Philadelphia, at 1434 Springfield Road, Collingdale, Delaware County, Pennsylvania.

- **1995** – The Anderson family home at 762 Martin Street was purchased by Blanch Burton-Lyles, Marian's protégée and the first Marian Anderson Scholarship Recipient. There she founded the National Marian Anderson Historical Society and

Museum which is headquartered in the original Anderson family residence.[1]

- **1997** – Centennial birthday tribute celebrations for Marian Anderson were held at Carnegie Hall and Union Baptist Church.

- **1998** – Philadelphia's Annual Marian Anderson Awards Gala at the Kimmel Center continues to honor critically acclaimed artists who have impacted society in a positive way, either through their work or their support for an important cause. Marian Anderson founded the Awards in 1942.

- **2018** – In November, Blanch Burton-Lyles died, passing on museum management to her protégée, Jillian Patricia Pirtle, who continues as CEO.

- **2019** – Filmmaker **Bill Nicoletti** wrote and produced *Once in a Hundred Years*, an award-winning PBS documentary of the life and musical legacy of Marian Anderson. https://www.youtube.com/watch?v=6VnbFtbo62M

- **2020** – The US Department of the Treasury scheduled issuance of new five-dollar bill picturing Marian Anderson, with Eleanor Roosevelt on the reverse side.

~As the most significant Philadelphian of the twentieth century, the legacy of Marian Anderson's voice, and her humanitarian contributions to our world must always be remembered and passed on to future generations ~

End Notes

1 **National Marian Anderson Historic Society Residence Museum** – 762 S. Martin Street, Philadelphia, PA 19146 (located between 19th–20th and Fitzwater Streets in Rittenhouse Square District). Tours by appointment only. Call (215)779-4219 or go online to http://marianandersonhistoricalsociety.weebly.com/museum-tours.html
2 Intentionally left blank
3 Today's value = #years to 2020 @ 4% using https://www.calculator.net/future-value-calculator.html
4 Undocumented but creditable anecdotal information in need of further research.

Appendix

Books about Marian Anderson

	TITLE	YEAR	AUTHOR
1	Marian Anderson: A Singer's Journey	2000	Allan Keiler
2	My Lord, What a Morning: An Autobiography	1956	Marian Anderson
3	Marian Anderson (Illustrator Seymeon Shimin, Hard cover)	1972	Tobi Tebias
4	The Voice that Challenged a Nation and the Struggle for Equal Rights	2011	Russell Freedman
5	Marian Anderson: A Life of Song	2005	Lisa Trumbauer
6	When Marian Sang: The True Recital of Marian Anderson (Illustrations by Brian Selznick)	2002	Pam Munoz Ryan

7	The Sound of Freedom: Marian Anderson – The Concert that Awakened America	2009	Raymond Arsonault
8	Marian Anderson (History Maker Bio Series)	2008	Jane Sutcliffe
9	Marian Anderson (Women of Achievement)	1988	Martina Horner and Anne Tedards
10	What I Had Was Singing: The Story of Marian Anderson	1994	Jeri Chase Ferris
11	Marian Anderson: A Great Singer (Great African American Series)	1991	Pat & Fredrick McKissak
12	Marian Anderson: Lady from Philadelphia	1965	Shirlee Petkin
13	Marian Anderson: Singer	1997	Anne Tedards
14	Marian Anderson: Album of Songs and Spirituals	1948	Marian Anderson, editor Franz Rupp
15	The Life of Marian Anderson: Diva and Humanitarian	2015	Andrea Broadwater
16	Women Who Dare Series: Marian Anderson	2007	Howard Kaplan
17	Marian Anderson (Impact Biographies)	1988	Charles Patterson
18	Marian Anderson: A Catalog of the Collection at the Univ. of Pennsylvania Library		Neda Westlake & Otto Albrecht, Edtors

19	Marian Anderson: A Portrait by Kosti Vehanen	1940s	Kosciusko Vehanen
20	Marian Anderson: A Voice Uplifted	2008	Victoria Garrett Jones
21	Marian Anderson: An Annotated Bibliography and Discography	1981	Compiled by Janet L. Sims
22	Marian Anderson By S. Hurok	1942	Sol Hurok
23	The Deep River Girl: The Life Story of Marian Anderson in Story	1949	Harry J. Albus

Photographs

A timeline of Marian Anderson's life:

Marian Anderson, one year old, in1898. (Strawbridge & Clothier Photographic Studios, Philadelphia)

John Berkley Anderson, Marian Anderson's father in the 1890s.

Marian Anderson, Anna Anderson, Alyse Anderson, Ethel Anderson after father's funeral in Philadelphia in January, 1910.

Marian Anderson receiving a large floral gift following her first concert at The Academy of Music in Philadelphia on April 22, 1918.

Marian Anderson (second from left–second row from top), with her Graduating Class from South Philadelphia High School for Girls in June, 1921. (Slutsky Studios, Philadelphia)

Marian Anderson, Helmer Enwall (Marian's Scandavian promoter) and Therese Enwall, at the Zoo in London, England in 1934.

Therese Enwall and Marian Anderson gathering hay in Finland in 1934.

Maestro Arturo Toscanini, the internationally acclaimed music personality with an eidetic memory, who proclaimed after hearing Marian Anderson in Salzburg in 1934, "what I heard today, one is privileged to hear only once in a hundred years."

Marian Anderson portrait used for U.S. Post Office stamp, Stockholm, Sweden, 1934. (Ben-Kow)

Marian Anderson and her Finnish accompanist, Kosti Vehanen performing at the Mozarteum in Salzburg, Austria in August, 1935.

Marian Anderson and Kosti Vehanen onboard the Ile de France, while returning to the United States during December, 1935.

Concert MARIAN ANDERSON
à l'Opéra de Paris, le 14 Décembre 1937

Marian Anderson singing at l'Opera de Paris, in Paris, France on December 14, 1937.

Giuseppe Boghetti, Marian Anderson's long-term voice coach, personally inscribed this picture on December 30, 1937.

Marian Anderson in the graduation procession at Howard University, Washington, D.C., prior to receiving her first, of over four-dozen honorary Doctorate Degrees from various Universities in June 1938.

Marian Anderson dressed and ready for her Lincoln Memorial concert in Washington DC on Easter Sunday April 9, 1939.

Marian Anderson with Kosti Vehanen, delivering the Historic Lincoln Memorial Concert to 75,000 people gathered on the National Mall in Washington, DC on April 9, 1939. (AP/Wide-World Photos)

Kosti Vehanen accompanying Marian Anderson while performing on the steps of the Lincoln Memorial in Washington DC on April 9, 1939.

Eleanor Roosevelt presenting the Spingarn Award to Marian Anderson at the annual meeting of the NAACP in Richmond, Virginia on July 2, 1939.

Marian Anderson kissing her mother, Anna, while receiving the Philadelphia Award (aka the Bok Award) on March 1, 1941.

Marian Anderson, an accomplished seemstress, at work using her Singer Sewing Machine at Marianna Farm in 1941.

Franz Rupp, Marian Anderson and Giuseppe Boghetti at Marianna Farm in 1941.

Marian Anderson christening the S.S. Booker T. Washington at Marin Shipyards in Sauaslito, CA on September 29, 1942.

Soldiers greeting Marian Anderson at Fort Logan Air Force Base, Colorado in March, 1943.

Marian Anderson on her knees praying at the alter in a Mexican Catholic Church during May or June, 1943.

Marian Anderson and Orpheus Fisher on their wedding day at Bethel Methodist Church in Danbury, Connecticut on July 17, 1943.

Duke Ellington and Marian Anderson meeting on May 7, 1944.

Marian Anderson performing as Leopold Stokowski, conducted the Westminster College Choir, New York City in December, 1944.

Marian Anderson with her dear friend, Dr. Albert Einstein, in the mid 1940s.

Marian Anderson with her manager of thirteen years, Sol Hurok, two months after Jackie Robinson's successful Major League Baseball debut, for which Hurok was also Jackie's Baseball Agent in June, 1947.	Marian Anderson rewarding her horse at Marianna Farm on October 1, 1949

Marian Anderson reupholstering an old chair at Marianna Farm in the Spring of 1951.

Marian Anderson cultivating her home vegetable garden at Mariana Farm during the Spring of 1951.

Anna Anderson sharing one of her delicious cooking secrets with her daughter, Marian, at Marianna Farm in the Spring of 1951.

Blanch Burton-Lyles' graduation from The Curtis Institute of Music in Philadelphia during the early 1950s.

Marian Anderson and Franz Rupp during a recording session at the RCA Victor Studio in New York City in the early 1950s.

Ed Sullivan and Marian Anderson chatting at CBS Studios in NYC on April 13, 1952.

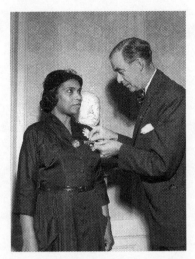

Marian Anderson receiving an award from King Gustav of Sweden in September, 1952.

Marian Anderson and Franz Rupp accepting flowers from children in Japan during May, 1953.

Marian Anderson with Franz Rupp entertaining wounded soldiers and local civilians onboard a hospital ship in Korea on May 30, 1953.

Marian Anderson at the original dedication of the Marian Anderson Recreation Center in Philadelphia in July, 1954. (Look Magazine)

Marian Anderson talking with a child at her childhood school, Stanton Elementary in Philadelphia in July, 1954. (Look Magazine)

Marian Anderson and her mother Anna, at the end of a busy day, relaxing on the front steps of their Martin Street home in Philadelphia in July 1954. (Look Magazine)

Marian Anderson with her youngest sister, Alyse Anderson, walking home to S. Martin Street in South Philadelphia in July, 1954. (Look Magazine)

Marian Anderson and Zinka Milanov, performing during Giuseppi Verdi's A Masked Ball, at the Metropolitan Opera House in New York City on January 7, 1955. (Sedge LeBlanc)

James De Preist, Anna Anderson (seated), Ethel De Preist, Alyse Anderson, outside the Anderson family home at 762 S. Martin Street, Philadelphia, ca. 1955.

Richard M. Nixon being sworn in as Vice President, following Marian Anderson [second row, front right] after she sang The National Anthem during President Eisenhower's second inauguration in Washington, DC on January 20, 1957.

Marian Anderson with dinner guests in Manila, Philippines in October, 1957.

Marian Anderson's arrival and greeting in Rangoon, Burma in October, 1957

Marian Anderson performing with the Bombay Symphony Orchestra in Bombay India, in November, 1957.

Marian Anderson singing at the Mahatma Gandhi Memorial in New Delhi, India in November, 1957.

Frederic R. Mann, Mayor Richardson Dilworth, Edward R. Murrow, Marian Anderson, James Magdanz, Donald W. Thornburgh in Philadelphia in late December, 1957.

Marian Anderson speaking during a discussion about the Cameroons in the Special Political and Decolonization Committee (aka the Fourth Committee) at the United Nations General Assembly in New York City, on November 12, 1958. (United Nations Photo Library).

Marian Anderson with Golda Meir, Prime Minister of Israel in New York City in 1958.

Marian Anderson with Eleanor Roosevelt on November 2, 1959.

Robert Kennedy and Marian Anderson on March 22, 1962.

Franz Rupp and Marian Anderson visiting with President John F. Kennedy at the White House in Washington, DC in March 1962.

Marian Anderson with Prince Reiner of Monaco and Princess Grace Kelly at the Philadelphia Museum of Art in Philadelphia on April 22, 1963.

Two weeks after President Kennedy's death President Johnson presents Marian Anderson with the Presidential Medal of Freedom, as Kennedy had originally planned to do, with Robert Kennedy in front row of the audience at the White House in Washington, DC on December 6, 1963.

Marian Anderson signing an autograph for her old friend, Nelson A. Rockefeller in the 1960s.

Marian Anderson leaving the stage after finishing her last career performance at Carnegie Hall on April 18, 1965.

Frederic R. Mann with Marian Anderson and her nephew James De Preist, Jr. at the Robin Hood Dell West (later renamed The Mann Music Center) on June 15, 1965.

Marian Anderson, Sponsor of the USS George Washington Carver (SSBN 656) with invited dignitaries prior to launch at Newport News Shipbuilding in Virginia on August 14, 1965.

Marian Anderson greeted by President Lyndon B. Johnson and Lady Bird Johnson [notice all eyes are on Marian] at the White House, Washington, DC on February 4, 1966.

Marian Anderson and her nephew James De Preist, Jr., ca. 1966.

Marian Anderson helping Girl Scouts sell cookies outside the Wanamaker Department Store in downtown Philadelphia in January, 1969.

Secretary of State Dean Rusk joshing with Marian Anderson and Senator Hubert H. Humphrey in the early 1970s.

James De Preist, Jr., Marian Anderson's nephew, Conductor of the Portland Symphony Orchestra, ca. 1970s.

Douglas Fairbanks Jr., personally autographed his picture to Marian Anderson as a "devoted fan," on March 23, 1976.

Marian Anderson rehearsing with Aaron Copeland, composer of 'A Lincoln Portrait,' at Saratoga Springs, New York in 1976.

Marian Anderson with Rosalynn Carter and President Jimmy Carter as he presented her with a Congressional Gold Medal at the White House in Washington, DC in August, 1978.

Marian Anderson being welcomed by Nelson A. Rockefeller to his family's estate at Pocantico Hills in New York on October 7, 1978.

Marian Anderson receiving yet another Doctorate Degree at the – at the age of ninety – from the University of Connecticut on June 6, 1987.

Marian Anderson at age ninety-two in 1989.

Marian Anderson visiting with Barbara Bush and President George Bush at the White House in Washington, DC on May 2, 1992.

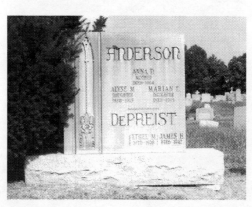

The Anderson family grave site, located on the left side of the main entrance road into Historic Eden Cemetery, 1434 Springfield Road, Collingdale, Delaware County, Pennsylvania USA

Printed in the United States
By Bookmasters